ARKANSAS SLAVE NARRATIVES

A Folk History of Slavery in Arkansas
from Interviews with Former Slaves

* * *

Typewritten records prepared by
THE FEDERAL WRITERS' PROJECT
1936-1938

* * *

Published in cooperation with
THE LIBRARY OF CONGRESS

APPLEWOOD BOOKS
Bedford, Massachusetts

The LIBRARY
of CONGRESS

A portion of the proceeds from the sale
of this book is donated to the Library of
Congress, which holds the original Slave
Narratives in its collection.

Thank you for purchasing an Applewood book.
Applewood reprints America's lively classics
--books from the past that are still of
interest to modern readers. For a free copy
of our current catalog, write to:

Applewood Books
P.O. Box 365
Bedford, MA 01730

ISBN 1-55709-011-4

FOREWORD

More than 140 years have elapsed since the ratification of the Thirteenth Amendment to the U.S. Constitution declared slavery illegal in the United States, yet America is still wrestling with the legacy of slavery. One way to examine and understand the legacy of the 19th Century's "peculiar institution" in the 21st century is to read and listen to the stories of those who actually lived as slaves. It is through a close reading of these personal narratives that Americans can widen their understanding of the past, thus enriching the common memory we share.

The American Folklife Center at the Library of Congress is fortunate to hold a powerful and priceless sampling of sound recordings, manuscript interviews, and photographs of former slaves. The recordings of former slaves were made in the 1930s and early 1940s by folklorists John A. and Ruby T. Lomax, Alan Lomax, Zora Neale Hurston, Mary Elizabeth Barnicle, John Henry Faulk, Roscoe Lews, and others. These aural accounts provide the only existing sound of voices from the institution of slavery by individuals who had been held in bondage three generations earlier. These voices can be heard by visiting the web site http://memory.loc.gov/ammem/collections/voices/. Added to the Folklife Center collections, many of the narratives from manuscript sources, which you find in this volume, were collected under the auspices of the United States Works Progress Administration (WPA), and were known as the slave narrative collection. These transcripts are found in the Library of Congress Manuscript Division. Finally, in addition to the Folklife Center photographs, a treasure trove of Farm Security Administration (FSA) photographs (including those of many former slaves) reside in the Prints and Photographs Division here at the nation's library. Together, these primary source materials on audio tape, manuscript and photographic formats are a unique research collection for all who would wish to study and understand the emotions, nightmares, dreams, and determination of former slaves in the United States.

The slave narrative sound recordings, manuscript materials, and photographs are invaluable as windows through which we can observe and be touched by the experiences of slaves who lived in the mid-19th century. At the same time, these archival materials are the fruits of an extraordinary documentary effort of the 1930s. The federal government, as part of its response to the Great Depression, organized unprecedented national initiatives to document the lives, experiences, and cultural traditions of ordinary Americans. The slave narratives, as documents of the Federal Writers Project, established and delineated our modern concept of "oral history." Oral history, made possible by the advent of sound recording technology, was "invented" by folklorists, writers, and other cultural documentarians under the aegis of the Library of Congress and various WPA offices—especially the Federal Writers' project—during the 1930s. Oral history has subsequently become both a new tool for the discipline of history, and a new cultural pastime undertaken in homes, schools, and communities by Americans of all walks of life. The slave narratives you read in the pages that follow stand as our first national exploration of the idea of oral history, and the first time that ordinary Americans were made part of the historical record.

The American Folklife Center has expanded upon the WPA tradition by continuing to collect oral histories from ordinary Americans. Contemporary projects such as our Veterans History Project, StoryCorps Project, Voices of Civil Rights Project, as well as our work to capture the stories of Americans after September 11, 2001 and of the survivors of Hurricanes Katrina and Rita, are all adding to the Library of Congress holdings that will enrich the history books of the future. They are the oral histories of the 21st century.

Frederick Douglas once asked: can "the white and colored people of this country be blended into a common nationality, and enjoy together...under the same flag, the inestimable blessings of life, liberty, and the pursuit of happiness, as neighborly citizens of a common country? I believe they can." We hope that the words of the former slaves in these editions from Applewood Books will help Americans achieve Frederick Douglas's vision of America by enlarging our understanding of the legacy of slavery in all of our lives. At the same time, we in the American Folklife Center and the Library of Congress hope these books will help readers understand the importance of oral history in documenting American life and culture—giving a voice to all as we create our common history.

Peggy A. Bulger

Peggy Bulger
Director, The American Folklife Center
Library of Congress

A NOTE FROM THE PUBLISHER

Since 1976, Applewood Books has been republishing books from America's past. Our mission is to build a picture of America through its primary sources. The book you hold in your hand is a testament to that mission. Published in cooperation with the Library of Congress, this collection of slave narratives is reproduced exactly as writers in the Works Progress Administration's Federal Writers' Project (1936–1938) originally typed them.

As publishers, we thought about how to present these documents. Rather than making them more readable by resetting the type, we felt that there was more value in presenting the narratives in their original form. We believe that to fully understand any primary source, one must understand the period of time in which the source was written or recorded. Collected seventy years after the emancipation of American slaves, these narratives had been preserved by the Library of Congress, fortunately, as they were originally created. In 1941, the Library of Congress microfilmed the typewritten pages on which the narratives were originally recorded. In 2001, the Library of Congress digitized the microfilm and made the narratives available on their American Memory web site. From these pages we have reproduced the original documents, including both the marks of the writers of the time and the inconsistencies of the type. Some pages were missing or completely illegible, and we have used a simple typescript provided by the Library of Congress so that the page can be read. Although the font occasionally can make these narratives difficult to read, we believe that it is important not only to preserve the narratives of the slaves but also to preserve the documents themselves, thereby commemorating the groundbreaking effort that produced them. That way, also, we can give you, the reader, not only a collection of the life stories of ex-slaves, but also a glimpse into the time in which these stories were collected, the 1930s.

These are powerful stories by those who lived through slavery. No institution was more divisive in American history than slavery. From the very founding of America and to the present day, slavery has touched us all. We hope these real stories of real lives are preserved for generations of Americans to come.

Please note: This volume is not the complete collection of narratives that were recorded for this state. The additional parts are available in additional volumes from Applewood Books. For the purposes of listing the narratives included in this book, we have provided the original typewritten contents page and placed a box around the narratives included in this volume.

INFORMANTS

Abbott, Silas	1	Benson, George		153
Abernathy, Lucian	3	Benton, Kato		155
Abromsom, Laura	8	Bertrand, James		157
Adeline, Aunt	11	Biggs, Alice		160
Adway, Rose	17	Billings, Mandy		162
Aiken, Liddie	19	Birch, Jane		164
Aldridge, Mattie	22	Black, Beatrice		166
Alexander, Amsy O.	24	Blackwell, Boston		168
Alexander, Diana	28	Blake, Henry		175
Alexander, Fannie	30	Blakeley, Adeline		180
Alexander, Lucretia	32	Bobo, Vera Roy		194
Allen, Ed	40	Boechus, Liddie		195
Allison, Lucindy	41	Bond, Maggie (Bunny)		197
Ames, Josephine	44	Bonds, Caroline		201
Anderson, Charles	46	Boone, Rev. Frank T.		202
Anderson, Nancy	49	Boone, J. F.		210
Anderson, R. B.	53	Boone, Jonas		214
Anderson, Sarah	55	Bowdry, John		216
Anderson, Selie	57	Boyd, Jack		218
Anderson, W. A.	60	Boyd, Mal		220
Anthony, Henry	62	Braddox, George	223,226	
Arbery, Katie	64	Bradley, Edward		229
Armstrong, Campbell	68	Bradley, Rachel		233
Armstrong, Cora	75	Brannon, Elizabeth		237
		Brantley, Mack		241
		Brass, Ellen		246
Baccus, Lillie	76	Bratton, Alice		249
Badgett, Joseph Samuel	78	Briles, Frank		251
Bailey, Jeff	84	Brooks, Mary Ann		253
Baker, James	91	Brooks, Waters		255
Baltimore, William	97	Brown, Casie Jones		267
Banks, Mose	101	Brown, Elcie		272
Banner, Henry	104	Brown, F. H.		275
Barnett, John W. H.	107	Brown, George		281
Barnett, Josephine Ann	109	Brown, J. N.		284
Barnett, Lizzie	112	Brown, Lewis	286,288,289	
Barnett, Spencer	115	Brown, Lewis		290
Barr, Emma	119	Brown, Mag		298
Barr, Robert	122	Brown, Mary		299
Bass, Matilda	126	Brown, Mattie		301
Beal, Emmett	127	Brown, Molly		303
Beard, Dina	129	Brown, Peter		311
Beck, Annie	131	Brown, William		315
Beckwith, J. H.	132	Brown, William		317
Beel, Enoch	135	Broyles, Maggie		324
Belle, Sophie D.	137	Bryant, Ida		329
Bellus, Cyrus	141	Buntin, Belle		330
Benford, Bob	146	Burgess, Jeff		334
Bennet, Carrie Bradley		Burkes, Norman		336
Logan	149	Burks, Sr., Will		338

Interviewer____Miss Irene Robertson____

Person Interviewed____Silas Abbott____
                                    R. F. D.
Age__73__   Brinkley, Ark.

- -

"I was born in Chickashaw County, Mississippi. Ely Abbott
and Maggie Abbott was our owners. They had three girls and two
boys - Eddie and Johnny. We played together till I was grown.
I loved em like if they was brothers. Papa and Mos Ely went to
war together in a two-horse top buggy. They both come back when
they got through.

"There was eight of us children and none was sold, none
give way. My parents name Peter and Mahaley Abbott. My father
never was sold but my mother was sold into this Abbott family
for a house girl. She cooked and washed and ironed. No'm, she
wasn't a wet nurse, but she tended to Eddie and Johnny and me
all alike. She whoop them when they needed, and Miss Maggie whoop
me. That the way we grow'd up. Mos Ely was 'ceptionly good I
recken. No'm, I never heard of him drinkin' whiskey. They made
cider and 'simmon beer every year.

"Grandpa was a soldier in the war. He fought in a battle.
I don't know the battle. He wasn't hurt. He come home and told
us how awful it was.

"My parents stayed on at Mos Ely's and my uncle's family
stayed on. He give my uncle a home and twenty acres of ground
and my parents same mount to run a gin. I drove two mules, my
brother drove two and we drove two more between us and run the

gin. My auntie seen somebody go in the gin one night but didn't think bout them settin' it on fire. They had a torch, I recken, in there. All I knowed, it burned up and Mos Ely had to take our land back and sell it to pay for four or five hundred bales of cotton got burned up that time. We stayed on and sharecropped with him. We lived between Egypt and Okolona, Mississippi. Aberdeen was our tradin' point.

"I come to Arkansas railroading. I railroaded forty years. Worked on the section, then I belong to the extra gang. I help build this railroad to Memphis.

"I did own a home but I got in debt and had to sell it and let my money go.

"Times is so changed and the young folks different. They won't work only nough to get by and they want you to give em all you got. They take it if they can. Nobody got time to work. I think times is worse than they ever been, cause folks hate to work so bad. I'm talking bout hard work, field work. Jobs young folks want is scarce; jobs they could get they don't want. They want to run about and fool around an get by.

"I get $8.00 and provisions from the government."

Interviewer   Watt McKinney

Person interviewed Lucian Abernathy, Marvell, Arkansas

Age 85

- -

"I was borned in de 'streme norf part of Mississippi nigh de Tennessee line. You mought say dat it was 'bout straddle of de state line and it wasn't no great piece from where us libed to Moscow what was de station on de ole Memfis en Charston Railroad. My white folks was de Abernathys. You neber do hear 'bout many folks wid dat name these times, leastwise not ober in dis state, but dere sure used to be heap of dem Abernathys back home where I libed and I spect dat mebbe some dere yit en cose it's bound to be some of the young uns lef' dar still, but de ole uns, Mars Luch en dem, dey is all gone.

"Mars Luch, he was my young boss. Though he name was Lucian us all called him Luch and dat was who I is named for. Ole mars, he was name Will and dat was Mars Luch's pa and my ole miss, she name Miss Cynthia and young miss, her name Miss Ellen. Ole mars an' ole miss, dey just had de two chillun, Mars Luch and Miss Ellen; dat is what libed to be grown. Mars Luch, he 'bout two year older dan me and Miss Ellen, she 'bout two year older dan Mars Luch. Miss Ellen, she married er gentman from Virginny and went dar to lib and Mars Luch, he married Miss Fannie Keith.

"Miss Fannie's folks, dey libed right nigh us on de 'j'ining place and dem was my ole man's peoples. Yas sah, boss, dat ole man you see settin' right dar now in dat chere. She was Ella Keith, dats zackly what her named when us married and she named for Miss Fannie's ma. Dat she was.

Us neber did leave our folkses eben atter de War ober and de niggers git dey freedom, yit an' still a heap of de niggers did leave dey mars' and a heap of dem didn' an' us stayed on en farmed de lan' jus' like us been doin' 'cept dey gib us a contract for part de crop an' sell us our grub 'gainst us part of de crop and take dey money outen us part of de cotton in de fall just like de bizness is done yit and I reckon dat was de startin' of de sharecrop dat is still goin' on.

"Soon atter Mars Luch good and grown an' him an' Miss Fannie done married, ole mars and ole miss, dey bofe died and Mars Luch say he gwine sell out an' lebe 'cause de lan' gittin' so poor and wore out and it takin' three an' more acres to make a bale and he tell us all dat when we wind up de crop dat fall and say, 'You boys mebbe can stay on wid whoever I sell out to er if not den you can fin' you homes wid some one close if you wants to do dat.' And den he says dat he gwine fin' him some good lan' mebbe in Arkansas down de riber from Memfis. Mighty nigh all de ole famblys lef' de place when Mars Luch sole it out.

"My pappy and my mammy, dey went to Memfis and me wid 'em. I was growed by den and was fixin' to marry Ella just es soon es I could fin' a good home. I was a country nigger en liked de farm an' en cose wasn't satisfied in town, so 'twasn't long 'fore I heered 'bout han's beein' needed down de riber in Mississippi and dats where I went en stayed for two years and boss, I sure was struck wid dat lan' what you could make a bale to a acre on an' I just knowed dat I was gwine git rich in a hurry an' so I writ er letter to Ella en her peoples tellin' dem 'bout de rich lan' and 'vising dem to come down dere where I was and I was wantin' to marry Ella den. Boss, and you know what, 'twasn't long afore I gits er letter back an' de letter says dat Ella an' her peoples is down de riber in Arkansas from Memfis

at Bledsoe wid Mars Luch an' Miss Fannie where Mars Luch had done moved him
an' Miss Fannie to a big plantation dey had bought down dere.

"Dat was a funny thing how dat happened an' Bledsoe, it was right
'cross de riber from where I was en had been for two years an' just soon es I
git dat letter I 'range wid a nigger to take me 'cross de riber in er skift
to de plantation where dey all was and 'bout fust folkses dat I see is Ella
an' her peoples en lots of de famblys from de ole home place back in Tennessee
an' I sure was proud to see Mars Luch en Miss Fannie. Dey had built dem-
selves a fine house at a p'int dat was sorter like a knoll where de water
don' git when de riber come out on de lan' in case of oberflow and up de rode
'bout half mile from he house. Mars Luch had de store en de gin. Dey had de
boys den, dat is Mars Luch and Miss Fannie did, and de boys was named Claude
an' Clarence atter Miss Fannie's two brudders.

"Dem was de finest boys dat one ever did see. At dat time Claude, he
'bout two year old and Clarence, he 'bout four er mebbe little less. Ella,
she worked in de house cooking for Miss Fannie an' nussin' de chillun and she
plumb crazy 'bout de chillun an' dey just as satisfied wid her as dey was wid
dere mama and Ella thought more dem chillun dan she did anybody. She just
crazy 'bout dem boys. Mars Luch, he gibe me job right 'way sort flunkying
for him and hostling at de lot an' barn and 'twasn't long den 'fore Ella and
me, us git married an' libe in a cabin dat Mars Luch had built in de back of
de big house.

"Us git 'long fine for more dan a year and Mars Luch, he raise plenty
cotton an' et times us ud take trip up to Memfis on de boat, on de Phil Allin
what was 'bout de finest boat on de riber in dem days and de one dat most
frequent put in at us landin' wid de freight for Mars Luch and den he most
ginally sont he cotton an' seed to Memfis on dis same Phil Allin.

"I jus' said, boss, dat us git 'long fine for more dan a year and us all mighty happy till Miss Fannie took sick an' died an' it mighty nigh killed Mars Luch and all of us and Mars Luch, he jus' droop for weeks till us git anxious 'bout him but atter while he git better and seem like mebbe he gwine git ober he sadness but he neber was like he used to be afore Miss Fannie died.

"Atter Miss Fannie gone, Mars Luch, he say, 'Ella, you an' Luch mus' mobe in de big house an' make you a bed in de room where de boys sleep, so's you can look atter 'em good, 'cause lots nights I gwine be out late at de gin an' store an' I knows you gwine take plumb good care of dem chillun.' An' so us fixed us bed in de big house an' de boys, dey sleeped right dar in dat room on dere bed where us could take care of 'em.

"Dat went on for 'bout two years an' den Mars Luch, he 'gun to get in bad health an' jus' wasted down like and den one night when he at de store he took down bad and dey laid him down on de bed in de back room where he would sleep on sich nights dat he didn' come home when he was so busy an' he sont a nigger on a mule for me to come up dar an' I went in he room an' Mars Luch, he say, 'Lissen, Luch, you is been a good faithful nigger an' Ella too, an' I is gonna die tonight and I wants you to send er letter to Miss Ellen in Virginny atter I is daid en tell her to come an' git de boys 'cause she is all de kin peoples dat dey habe lef' now cepn cose you an' Ella an' it mought be some time afore she gits here so you all take good en faithful care dem till she 'rives an' tell her she habe to see dat all de bizness wind up and take de boys back wid her an' keep dem till dey is growed.'

"Well, boss, us done jus' like Mars Luch tell us to do an' us sure feel sorry for dem two little boys. Dey jus' 'bout five an' seben year old den and dey sure loved dere pa; dey was plumb crazy 'bout Mars Luch and him 'bout dem too.

" 'Bout two weeks from time dat Mars Luch daid, Miss Ellen come on de boat one night an' she stayed some days windin' up de bizness and den she lef' an' take de boys 'way wid her back to Virginny where she libed. Us sure did hate to 'part from dem chillun. Dat's been nigh on to sixty years ago but us neber forgit dem boys an' us will allus lobe dem. Dey used to sen' us presents an' sich every Christmas for seberal years and den us started movin' 'bout an' I reckon dey don' know where we's at now. I sure would like to see dem boys ag'in. I betcha I'd know dem right today. Mebbe I wouldn't, it's been so long since I seen 'em; but shucks, I know dat dey would know me."

Interviewer _____ Miss Irene Robertson _____

Person interviewed Laura Abromsom, R.F.D., Holly Grove, Arkansas
                        Receives mail at Clarendon, Arkansas

Age   74

- -

"My mama was named Eloise Rogers. She was born in Missouri. She was
sold and brought to three or four miles from Brownsville, Tennessee. Alex
Rogers bought her and my papa. She had been a house girl and well cared
for. She never got in contact wid her folks no more after she was sold.
She was a dark woman. Papa was a ginger cake colored man. Mama talked like
Alex Rogers had four or five hundred acres of land and lots of niggers to
work it. She said he had a cotton factory at Brownsville.

"Mistress Barbara Ann was his wife. They had two boys and three girls.
One boy George went plumb crazy and outlived 'em all. The other boy died
early. Alex Rogers got my papa in Richmond, Virginia. He was took outer a
gang. We had a big family. I have eight sisters and one brother.

"Pa say they strop 'em down at the carriage house and give 'em five
hundred lashes. He say they have salt and black pepper mixed up in er old
bucket and put it all on flesh cut up with a rag tied on a stick (mop).
Alex Rogers had a nigger to put it on the place they whooped. The Lord puts
up wid such wrong doings and den he comes and rectifies it. He does that
very way.

"Pa say they started to whoop him at the gin house. He was a sorter
favorite. He cut up about it. That didn't make no difference 'bout it.
Somehow they scared him up but he didn't git whooped thater time.

"They fed good on Alex Rogers' place. They'd buy a barrel of coffee, a
barrel molasses, a barrel sugar. Some great big barrels.

"Alex Rogers wasn't a good man. He'd tell them to steal a hog and git home wid it. If they ketch you over there they'll whoop you. He'd help eat hogs they'd steal.

"One time papa was working on the roads. The neighbor man and road man was fixing up their eating. He purty nigh starved on that road work. He was hired out.

"Mama and papa spoke like they was mighty glad to get sat free. Some believed they'd git freedom and others didn't. They had places they met and prayed for freedom. They stole out in some of their houses and turned a washpot down at the door. Another white man, not Alex Rogers, tole mama and papa and a heap others out in the field working. She say they quit and had a regular bawl in the field. They cried and laughed and hollered and danced. Lot of them run offen the place soon as the man tole 'em. My folks stayed that year and another year.

"What is I been doing? Ast me is I been doing? What ain't I been doing be more like it. I raised fifteen of my own children. I got four living. I living wid one right here in dis house wid me now. I worked on the farm purty nigh all my life. I come to dis place. Wild, honey, it was! I come in 1901. Heap of changes since then.

"Present times—Not as much union 'mongst young black and white as the old black and white. They growing apart. Nobody got nothin' to give. No work. I used to could buy second-handed clothes to do my little children a year for a little or nothin'. Won't sell 'em now nor give 'em 'way neither. They don't work hard as they used to. They say they don't git nothin' outen it. They don't want to work. Times harder in winter 'cause it cold and things to eat killed out. I cans meat. We dry beef. In town this Nickellodian playing wild wid young colored folks—these Sea Bird music boxes.

They play all kind things. Folks used to stay home Saturday nights. Too much running 'round, excitement, wickedness in the world now. This generation is worst one. They trying to cut the Big Apple dance when we old folks used to be down singing and praying. 'Cause dis is a wicked age times is bad and hard."

Interviewer's Comment

Mulatto, clean, intelligent.

Interviewer_____ Mrs. Zillah Cross Peel

Person interviewed_____ "Aunt Adeline"_____ Age__89__

Home_____ 101 Rock Street, Fayetteville, Arkansas _____

- -

"I was born a slave about 1848, in Hickmon County, Tennessee," said Aunt Adeline who lives as care taker in a house at 101 Rock Street, Fayetteville, Arkansas, which is owned by the Blakely-Hudgens estate.

Aunt Adeline has been a slave and a servant in five generations of the Parks family. Her mother, Liza, with a group of five Negroes, was sold into slavery to John P. A. Parks, in Tennessee, about 1840.

"When my mother's master came to Arkansas about 1849, looking for a country residence, he bought what was known as the old Kidd place on the Old Wire Road, which was one of the Stage Coach stops. I was about one year old when we came. We had a big house and many times passengers would stay several days and wait for the next stage to come by. It was then that I earned my first money. I must have been about six or seven years old. One of Mr. Parks' daughters was about one and a half years older than I was. We had a play house back of the fireplace chimney. We didn't have many toys; maybe a doll made of a corn cob, with a dress made from scraps and a head made from a roll of scraps. We were playing church. Miss Fannie was the preacher and I was the audience. We were singing "Jesus my all to Heaven is gone."

When we were half way through with our song we discovered that the passengers from the stage coach had stopped to listen. We were so frightened at our audience that we both ran. But we were coaxed to come back for a dime and sing our song over. I remember that Miss Fannie used a big leaf for a book.

"I had always been told from the time I was a small child that I was a Negro of African stock. That it was no disgrace to be a Negro and had it not been for the white folks who brought us over here from Africa as slaves, we would never have been here and would have been much better off.

"We colored folks were not allowed to be taught to read or write. It was against the law. My master's folks always treated me well. I had good clothes. Sometimes I was whipped for things I should not have done just as the white children were.

"When a young girl was married her parents would always give her a slave. I was given by my master to his daughter, Miss Elizabeth, who married Mr. Blakely. I was just five years old. She moved into a new home at Fayetteville and I was taken along but she soon sent me back home to my master telling him that I was too little and not enough help to her. So I went back to the Parks home and stayed until I was over seven years old. *My master made a bill of sale for me to his daughter, in order to keep account of all settlements, so when he died and the estate settled each child would know how he stood.

- -

*This statement can be verified by the will made by John P. A. Parks, and filed in Probate Court in the clerk's office in Washington County.

"I was about 15 years old when the Civil War ended and was still living with Mrs. Blakely and helped care for her little children. Her daughter, Miss Lenora, later married H. M. Hudgens, and I then went to live with her and cared for her children. When her daughter Miss Helen married Professor Wiggins, I took care of her little daughter, and this made five generations that I have cared for.

"During the Civil War, Mr. Parks took all his slaves and all of his fine stock, horses and cattle and went South to Louisiana following the Southern army for protection. Many slave owners left the county taking with them their slaves and followed the army.

"When the war was over, Mr. Parks was still in the South and gave to each one of his slaves who did not want to come back to Arkansas so much money. My uncle George came back with Mr. Parks and was given a good mountain farm of forty acres, which he put in cultivation and one of my uncle's descendents still lives on the place. My mother did not return to Arkansas but went on to Joplin, Missouri, and for more than fifty years, neither one of us knew where the other one was until one day a man from Fayetteville went into a restaurant in Joplin and ordered his breakfast, and my mother who was in there heard him say he lived in Fayetteville, Arkansas. He lived just below the Hudgens home and when my mother enquired about the family he told her I was still alive and was with the family. While neither of us could read nor write we corresponded through different people. But I never saw her after I was eleven years old. Later Mr. Hudgens went to Joplin to see if she was well taken care of. She owned her own little place and when she died there was enough money for her to be buried.

"Civil War days are vivid to me. The Courthouse which was then in the middle of the Square was burned one night by a crazy Confederate soldier. The old men in the town saved him and then put him in the county jail to keep him from burning other houses. Each family was to take food to him and they furnished bedding. The morning I was to take his breakfast, he had ripped open his feather bed and crawled inside to get warm. The room was so full of feathers when I got there that his food nearly choked him. I had carried him ham, hot biscuits and a pot of coffee.

"After the War many soldiers came to my mistress, Mrs. Blakely, trying to make her free me. I told them I was free but I did not want to go anywhere, that I wanted to stay in the only home that I had ever known. In a way that placed me in a wrong attitude. I was pointed out as different. Sometimes I was threatened for not leaving but I stayed on.

"I had always been well treated by my master's folks. While we lived at the old Kidd place, there was a church a few miles from our home. My uncle George was coachman and drove my master's family in great splendor in a fine barouche to church. After the war, when he went to his own place, Mr. Parks gave him the old carriage and bought a new one for the family.

"I can remember the days of slavery as happy ones. We always had an abundance of food. Old Aunt Martha cooked and there was always plenty prepared for all the white folks as well as the colored folks. There was a long table at the end of the big kitchen for the colored folks. The vegetables were all prepared of an evening by Aunt Martha with someone to help her.

"My mother seemed to have a gift of telling fortunes. She had a
brass ring about the size of a dollar with a handwoven knotted string
that she used. I remember that she told many of the young people in
the neighborhood many strange things. They would come to her with
their premonitions.

"Yes, we were afraid of the patyroles. All colored folks were.
They said that any Negroes that were caught away from their master's
premises without a permit would be whipped by the patyroles. They used
to sing a song:

> 'Run nigger run,
>
> The patyroles
>
> Will get you.'

"Yes'm, the War separated lots of families. Mr. Parks' son, John
C. Parks, enlisted in Colonel W. H. Brooks' regiment at Fayetteville as
third lieutenant. Mr. Jim Parks was killed at the Battle of Getys-
burg.

"I do remember it was my mistress, Mrs. Blakely, who kept the
Masonic Building from being burned. The soldiers came to set it on
fire. Mrs. Blakely knew that if it burned, our home would burn as it
was just across the street. Mrs. Blakely had two small children who
were very ill in upstairs rooms. She told the soldiers if they burned
the Masonic Building that her house would burn and she would be unable
to save her little children. They went away."

While Aunt Adeline is nearing ninety, she is still active, goes
shopping and also tends to the many crepe myrtle bushes as well as
many other flowers at the Hudgens place.

She attends to the renting of the apartment house, as caretaker, and is taken care of by members of the Blakely-Hudgens families.

Aunt Adeline talks "white folks language," as they say, and seldom associates with the colored people of the town.

Interviewer_____Mrs. Bernice Bowden

Person interviewed_____Rose Adway
  405 W. Pullen, Pine Bluff, Arkansas

Age___76___

- -

"I was born three years 'fore surrender. That's what my people told me. Born in Mississippi. Let me see what county I come out of. Smith County--that's where I was bred and born.

"I know I seen the Yankees but I didn't know what they was. My mama and papa and all of 'em talked about the War.

"My papa was a water toter in durin' the War. No, he didn't serve the army--just on the farm.

"Mama was the cook for her missis in slavery times.

"I think my folks went off after freedom and then come back. That was after they had done been sot free. I can remember dat all right.

"I registered down here at the Welfare and I had to git my license from Mississippi and I didn't remember which courthouse I got my license, but I sont letters over there till I got it up. I got all my papers now, but I ain't never got no pension.

"I been through so much I can't git much in my remembrance, but I was here--that ain't no joke--I been here.

"My folks said their owners was all right. You know they was 'cause they come back. I remember dat all right.

"I been farmin' till I got disabled. After I married I went to farmin'. And I birthed fourteen head of chillun by dat one man! Fourteen head by dat one man! Stayed at home and took care of 'em till I got 'em up some size, too. All dead but five out of the fourteen head.

"My missis' name was Miss Catherine and her husband named Abe Carr.

"I went to school a little bit—mighty little. I could read but I never could write.

"And I'm about to go blind in my old age. I need help and I need it bad. Chillun ain't able to help me none 'cept give me a little bread and give me some medicine once in a while. But I'm thankful to the Lord I can get outdoors.

"I don't know what to think of this young race. That baby there knows more than I do now, nearly. Back there when I was born, I didn't know nothin'.

"I know they said it was bad luck to bring a hoe or a ax in the house on your shoulder. I heard the old folks tell dat—sure did.

"And I was told dat on old Christmas night the cows gets down on their knees and gives thanks to the Lord.

"I 'member one song:

> 'I am climbin' Jacob's ladder
> I am climbin' Jacob's ladder
> I am climbin' Jacob's ladder
> For the work is almost done.
>
> 'Every round goes higher and higher
> Every round goes higher and higher
> Every round goes higher and higher
> For my work is almost done.
>
> 'Sister, now don't you get worried
> Sister, now don't you get worried
> Sister, now don't you get worried
> For the work is almost done.'

My mother used to sing dat when she was spinnin' and cardin'. They'd spin and dye the thread with some kind of indigo. Oh, I 'member dat all right."

Interviewer_____Miss Irene Robertson

Person interviewed_____Liddie Aiken, Wheatley, Arkansas

Age 62

- -

"My mother was born in southwest Georgia close to the Alabama line. Her mother come from Virginia. She was sold with her mother and two little brothers. Her mother had been sold and come in a wagon to southwest Georgia. They was all field hands. They cleaned out new ground. They was afraid of hoop-snakes. She said they look like a hoop rolling and whatever they stuck a horn or their tail in it died. They killed trees.

"Mama said she druther plough than chop. She was a big woman and they let her plough right along by her two little brothers, Henry and Will Keller. Will et so many sweet potatoes they called him 'Tater Keller.' After he got grown we come out here. Folks called him 'Tate Keller.' Henry died. I recollect Uncle Tate.

"I was born close to Mobile, Alabama. Mama was named Sarah Keller. Grandma was called Mariah. Banks Tillman sold her the first time. Bill Keller bought them all the last time. His wife was named Ada Keller. They had a great big family but I forgot what they said about them. Mack clem up in a persimmon tree one day and the old man hollered at him, 'Get out of that tree 'fore you fall.' 'Bout then the boy turned 'loose and fell. It knocked the breath out him. It didn't kill him. Three or four of Miss Ada's children died with congestive chills. Mama said the reason they had them chills they played down at the gin pond all the time. It was shady and a pretty place and they was allowed to play in the pond. Three or four of them died nearly in a heap.

"One of the boys had a pet billy-goat. It got up on top mama's house one time. It would bleat and look down at them. They was afraid it would jump down on them if they went out. It chewed up things Aunt Beanie washed. She had them put out on bushes and might had a line too. They fattened it and killed it. Mama said Mr. Bill Keller never had nothing too good to divide with his niggers. I reckon by that they got some of the goat.

"They lived like we live now. Every family done his own cooking. I don't know how many families lived on the place.

"I know about the Yankees. They come by and every one of the men and boys went with them but Uncle Cal. He was cripple and they advised him not to start. Didn't none of the women go. Mama said she never seen but one ever come back. She thought they got killed or went on some place else.

"Mr. Keller died and Miss Ada went back to her folks. They left everything in our care that they didn't move. She took all her house things. They sold or took all their stock. They left us a few cows and pigs. I don't know how long they stayed after the old man died. His children was young; he might not been so old.

"I recollect grandma. She smoked a pipe nearly all the time. My papa was a livery stable man. He was a fine man with stock. He was a little black man. Mama was too big. Grandma was taller but she was slick black. He lived at Mobile, Alabama. I was the onliest child mama had. Uncle 'Tate Keller' took grandma and mama to Mobile. He never went to the War. He was a good carpenter and he worked out when he didn't have a lot to do in the field. He was off at work when all the black men and boys left Mr. Bill. He never went back after they left till freedom.

"They didn't know when freedom took place. They was all scattering for two years about to get work and something to eat.

Tate come and got them. They went off in a wagon that Tate made for his master, Bill Keller. We come to Tupelo, Mississippi from Mobile when I was a little bit of a girl. Then we made one crop and come to Helena. Uncle Tate died there and mama died at Crocketts Bluff. My papa died back in Mobile, Alabama. He was breaking a young horse and got throwed up side a tree. He didn't live long then.

"I got three boys now and I had seben--all boys. They farms and do public work. Tom is in Memphis. Pete is in Helena and I live wid Macon between here (Wheatley) and Cotton Plant. We farm. I done everything could be thought of on a farm. I ploughed some less than five year ago. I liked to plough. My boy ploughs all he can now and we do the chopping. We all pick cotton and get in the corn. We work day laborers now.

"If I was young the times wouldn't stand in my way. I could make it. I don't know what is the trouble lessen some wants too much. They can't get it. We has a living and thankful for it. I never 'plied for no help yet.

"I still knits my winter stockings. I got knitting needles and cards my own mother had and used. I got use for them. I wears clothes on my body in cold weather. One reason you young folks ain't no 'count you don't wear enough clothes when it is cold. I wear flannel clothes if I can get holt of them.

"Education done ruint the world. I learnt to read a little. I never went to school. I learnt to work. I learnt my boys to go with me to the field and not to be ashamed to sweat. It's healthy. They all works."

Interviewer_____Miss Irene Robertson_____

Person Interviewed_____Mattie Aldridge_____

Age 60?_____Hazen, Arkansas_____

- -

"My mother's old owner named Master Sanders. She born somewhere in Tennessee. I heard her say she lived in Mississippi. I was born in Tennessee. My pa was born in Mississippi. I know he belong to the Duncans. His name George Washington Duncan. There ain't nary drap white blood in none us. I got four brothers. I do remembers grandma. She set and tell us tales bout old times like you want to know. Been so long I forgotten. Ma was a house girl and pa a field hand. Way grandma talked it must of been hard to find out what white folks wanted em to do, cause she couldn't tell what you say some times. She never did talk plain.

"They was glad when freedom declared. They said they was hard on em. Whoop em. Pa was killed in Crittenden County in Arkansas. He was clearin' new ground. A storm come up and a limb hit him. It killed him. Grandma and ma allus say like if you build a house you want to put all the winders in you ever goin' to want. It bad luck to cut in and put in nother one. Sign of a death. I ain't got no business tellin' you bout that. White folks don't believe in signs.

"I been raisin' up childern - 'dopted childern, washin', ironin', scourin', hoein', gatherin' corn, pickin' cotton, patchin', cookin'. They ain't nothin' what I ain't done.

"No'm, I sure ain't voted. I don't believe in women votin'. They don't know who to vote for. The men don't know neither. If folks visited they would care more bout the other an wouldn't be so much devilment goin' on."

Interviewer   Samuel S. Taylor

Person Interviewed   Amsy O. Alexander
        2422 Center Street, Little Rock, Arkansas

Age 74

[_p. Bula adress_]

- -

"I was born in the country several miles from Charlotte in Macklenberg, County, North Carolina in 1854.

"My father's name was John Alexander and my mother was Esther McColley. That was her maiden name of course.

"My father's master was named Silas Alexander and my mother belonged to Hugh Reed. I don't know just how she and my father happened to meet. These two slaveholders were adjoining neighbors, you might say.

"My father and my mother married during the war. I was the first child. I had three half brothers and three half sisters from the father's side. I didn't have no whole brothers and sisters. I am the only one on my mother's side. My father was not in the war.

"I don't know that the pateroles bothered him very much. My father and mother were well treated by our master and then both she and my father were quiet and their masters were good to them naturally.

"During slavery times, my father was a farmer. My mother farmed too. She was a hand in the field. They lived in a little log cabin, one room. They had a bed in there, a few chairs and a homemade table. They had a plank floor. I only know what I heard my people speak of. I don't know what was what for myself because I was too young.

"From what I can understand they had a big room at the house and the slaves came there and ate there. They had a colored woman who prepared their meals. The children mostly were raised on pot liquor. While the old folk were working the larger young uns mongst the children would take care of the little ones.

"Their masters never forced any breeding. I have heard of that happening in other places but I never heard them speak of it in connection with our master.

"When the master came back from the war, they told the slaves they were free. After slavery my people stayed on and worked on the old plantation. They didn't get much. Something like fifty cents a day and one meal. My folks didn't work on shares.

"Back there in North Carolina times got tight and it seemed that there wasn't much doing. Agents came from Arkansas trying to get laborers. So about seven or eight families of us emigrated from North Carolina. That is how my folks got here.

"The Ku Klux were bad in North Carolina too. My people didn't have any trouble with them in Arkansas, though. They weren't bothered so much in North Carolina because of their owners. But they would come around and see them. They came at night. We came to Arkansas in the winter of 1897.

"I went to public school after the war, in North Carolina. I didn't get any further than the eighth grade. My father and mother didn't get any schooling till after the war. They could read a little but they picked it up themselves during slavery. I suppose their Master's children learned it to them.

"My father never did see any army service. I have heard him speak of seeing soldiers come through though. They looted the place and took everything they wanted and could carry.

"When I first come to this state, I settled in Drew County and farmed. I farmed for three years. During the time I was there, I got down sick

with slow fever. When I got over that I decided that I would move to higher
ground. There was a man down there who recommended Little Rock and so I
moved here. I have been here forty-nine years. That is quite a few days.

"I belong to the Presbyterian Church and have been a member of that church
for fifty-five years. I have never gotten out publicly, but I even do my
little preaching round in the house here.

"When I came to Little Rock, I came in a very dull season. There wasn't
even a house to be rented. It was in the winter. I had to rent a room at
"Jones" hall on Ninth and Gaines streets and paid one dollar a day for it.
I stayed there about a month. Finally there was a vacant house over on Nine-
teenth street and Common and I moved there. Then I commenced to look for
work and I walked the town over daily. No results whatever. Finally I struck
a little job with the contractor here digging ditches, grubbing stumps, grad-
ing streets and so forth. I worked with him for three years and finally I
got a job with the street car company, as laborer in the Parks. I worked at
that job two years. Finally I got a job as track laborer. I worked there a
year. Then I was promoted to track foreman. I held that seven years.

- "I quit that then and went to the railroads. I helped to build the Choc-
taw Oklahoma and Gulf Railway. When the road was completed, I made the first
trip over it as Porter. I remained there till August 9, 1928. During that
time I was operated on for prostatitis and doctors rendered me unfit for work,
totally disabled; so that is my condition today.

"I think the future looks bright. I think conditions will get better.
I believe that all that is necessary for betterment is cooperation.

"I believe the younger generation -- the way it looks -- is pretty bad.
I think we haven't done anything like as much as we could do in teaching
the youngsters. We need to give them an idea of things. They don't know.

Our future depends on our children. If their minds aren't trained, the future will not be bright. Our leaders should lecture to these young people and teach them. We have young people who dodge voting because of the poll tax. That is not the right attitude. I don't know what will become of us if our children are not better instructed. The white people are doing more of this than we are.

There was a time when children didn't know but what the foot was all there was of a chicken. The foot was all they had ever seen. But young folks nowaday should be taught everything.

Interviewer_____Miss Irene Robertson_____

Person interviewed_____Diana Alexander, Brinkley, Arkansas_____

Age___74___

- -

"I was born in Mississippi close to Bihalia. Our owner was Myers (?) Bogan. He had a wife and children. Mama was a field woman. Her name was Sarah Bogan and papa's name was Hubbard Bogan.

"I heard them talk about setting the pot at the doors and having singing and prayer services. They all sung and prayed around the room. I forgot all the things they talked about. My parents lived on the same place after freedom a long time. They said he was good to them.

"Dr. Bogan in Forrest City, Arkansas always said I was his brother's child. He was dead years ago, so I didn't have no other way of knowing.

"The only thing I can recollect about the War was once my mistress took me and her own little girl upstairs in a kind of ceiling room (attic). They had their ham meat and jewelry locked up in there and other fine stuff. She told us to sit down and not move, not even grunt. Me and Fannie had to be locked up so long. It was dark. We both went to sleep but we was afraid to stir. The Yankees come then but I didn't get to see them. I didn't want to be took away by 'em. I was big enough to know that. I heard 'em say we was near 'bout eat out at the closing of the War. I thought it muster been the Yankees from what they was talking about, eating us out.

"I been washing and ironing and still doing it. All my life I been doing that 'ceptin' when I worked in the field.

"Me and my daughter is paying on this house (a good house). I been making my own living--hard or easy. I don't get no relief aid. Never have. I 'plied for the old people's pension. Don't get it."

Interviewer's Comment

This must be Myers Bogan, yet she told me Bogan Myers. Later she said Dr. Bogan of Forrest City was thus and so.

Interviewer_____Miss Irene Robertson_____

Person interviewed_____Fannie Alexander, Helena, Arkansas_____

Age___62___

- -

"I was an orphant child. My mother-in-law told me during slavery she
was a field hand. One day the overseer was going to whoop one of the women
'bout sompin or other and all the women started with the hoes to him and run
him clear out of the field. They would killed him if he hadn't got out of
the way. She said the master hadn't put a overseer over them for a long
time. Some of 'em wouldn't do their part and he put one of the men on the
place over the women. He was a colored foreman. The women worked together
and the men worked together in different fields. My mother-in-law was named
Alice Drummond. She said they would cut the hoecakes in half and put that
in your pan, then pour the beef stew on top. She said on Christmas day they
had hot biscuits. They give them flour and things to make biscuit at home
on Sundays. When they got through eating they take their plate and say,
'Thank God for what I received.' She said they had plenty milk. The churns
was up high--five gallon churns. Some churns was cedar wood. The children
would churn standing on a little stool. It would take two to churn. They
would change about and one brushed away the flies. She lived close to
Meridian and Canton.

"My mother talked the bright side to her children. She was born
in Tennessee. She had two older sisters sold from her. She never
seen them no more. They was took to Missouri. Mother was never
sold. She was real bright color. She died when I was real little.

From what I know I think my parents was industrious. Papa was a shoemaker. He worked on Sunday to make extra money to buy things outside of what his master give them for his family. Now I can remember that much. My papa was a bright color like I am but not near as light as mama. He had a shop when I was little but he wasn't 'lowed to keep it open on Sunday. I heard him tell about working on Sundays during slavery and how much he made sometimes. He tanned his own leather.

"I went to Mississippi and married. Folks got grown earlier than they do now and I married when I was a young girl 'bout seventeen. We come to Arkansas. I sewed for white and colored. I cooked some. I taught school in the public schools. I taught opportunity school two years. I had a class at the church in day and at the schoolhouse at night. I had two classes.

"John Hays was mama's owner in Tennessee."

300333

Interviewer _____ Samuel S. Taylor _____

Person interviewed _____ Lucretia Alexander _____
                    1708 High Street, Little Rock, Arkansas

Age   89

- -

"I been married three times and my last name was Lucretia Alexander.
I was twelve years old when the War began. My mother died at seventy-three
or seventy-five. That was in August 1865---August the ninth. She was
buried August twelfth. The reason they kept her was they had refugeed her
children off to different places to keep them from the Yankees. They
couldn't get them back. My mother and her children were heir property.
Her first master was Toliver. My mother was named Agnes Toliver. She had
a boy and a girl both older than I were. My brother come home in '65. I
never got to see my sister till 1869.

"My father died in 1881 and some say he was one hundred twelve and
some say one hundred six. His name was Beasley, John Beasley, and he went
by John Beasley till he died.

"My mother died and left four living children. I was the youngest.

"I got religion in 1865. I was baptized seventy-three years ago this
August.

"I ain't got nary living child. My oldest child would have been sixty-
four if he were living. They claim my baby boy is living, but I don't know.
I have four children.

"The first overseer I remember was named Kurt Johnson. The next was
named Mack McKenzie. The next one was named Pink Womack. And the next was
named Tom Phipps. Mean! Liked meanness! Mean a man as he could be. I've
seen him take them down and whip them till the blood run out of them.

"I got ten head of grandchildren. And I been grandmother to eleven head. I been great-grandmother to twelve head of great-grandchildren. I got one twenty-three and another nineteen or twenty. Her father's father was in the army. She is the oldest. Lotas Robinson, my granddaughter, has four children that are my great-grandchildren. Gayden Jenkins, my grandson, has two girls. I got a grandson named Dan Jenkins. He is the father of three boys. He lives in Cleveland. He got a grandson named Mark Jenkins in Memphis who has one boy. The youngest granddaughter—I don't remember her husband's name—has one boy. There are four generations of us.

"I been here. You see I took care of myself when I was young and tried to do right. The Lord has helped me too. Yes, I am going on now. I been here a long time but I try to take care of myself. I was out visiting the sick last time you come here. That's the reason I missed you. I tries to do the best I can.

"I am stricken now with the rheumatism on one side. This hip.

"My mother was treated well in slavery times. My father was sold five times. Wouldn't take nothin'. So they sold him. They beat him and knocked him about. They put him on the block and they sold him 'bout beatin' up his master. He was a native of Virginia. The last time they sold him they sold him down in Claiborne County, Mississippi. Just below where I was born at. I was born in Copiah County near Hazlehurst, about fifteen miles from Hazlehurst. My mother was born in Washington County, Virginia. Her first master was Qualls Tolliver. Qualls moved to Mississippi and married a woman down there and he had one son, Peachy Toliver. After he died, he willed her to Peachy. Then Peachy went to the Rebel army and got killed.

"My mother's father was a free Indian named Washington. Her mother was a slave. I don't know my father's father. He moved about so much and was sold so many times he never did tell me his father. He got his name from the white folks. When you're a slave you have to go by your owner's name.

"My master's mother took me to the house after my mother died. And the first thing I remember doing was cleaning up. Bringing water, putting up mosquito-bars, cooking. My master's mother was Susan Rewd. I have done everything but saw. I never sawed in my life. The hardest work I did was after slavery. I never did no hard work during slavery. I used to pack water for the plow hands and all such as that. But when my mother died, my mistress took me to the house.

"But Lawd! I've seen such brutish doin's---runnin' niggers with hounds and whippin' them till they was bloody. They used to put 'em in stocks. When they didn't put 'em in stocks, used to be two people would whip 'em--- the overseer and the driver. The overseer would be a man named Elijah at our house. He was just a poor white man. He had a whip they called the BLACK SNAKE.

"I remember one time they caught a man named George Tinsley. They put the dogs on him and they bit 'im and tore all his clothes off of 'im. Then they put 'im in the stocks. The stocks was a big piece of timber with hinges in it. It had a hole in it for your head. They would lift it up and put your head in it. There was holes for your head, hands and feet in it. Then they would shut it up and they would lay that whip on you and you couldn't do nothin' but wiggle and holler, 'Pray, master, pray!' But when they'd let that man out, he'd run away again.

"They would make the slaves work till twelve o'clock on Sunday, and then they would let them go to church. The first time I was sprinkled, a white preacher did it; I think his name was Williams.

"The preacher would preach to the white folks in the forenoon and to the colored folks in the evening. The white folks had them hired. One of them preachers was named Hackett; another, Williams; and another, Gowan. There was five of them but I just remember them three. One man used to hold the slaves so late that they had to go to the church dirty from their work. They would be sweaty and smelly. So the preacher 'buked him 'bout it. That was old man Bill Rose.

"The niggers didn't go to the church building; the preacher came and preached to them in their quarters. He'd just say, 'Serve your masters. Don't steal your master's turkey. Don't steal your master's chickens. Don't steal your master's hawgs. Don't steal your master's meat. Do what-someever your master tells you to do.' Same old thing all the time.

"My father would have church in dwelling houses and they had to whisper. My mother was dead and I would go with him. Sometimes they would have church at his house. That would be when they would want a real meetin' with some real preachin'. It would have to be durin' the week nights. You couldn't tell the difference between Baptists and Methodists then. They was all Christians. I never saw them turn nobody down at the communion, but I have heard of it. I never saw them turn no pots down neither; but I have heard of that. They used to sing their songs in a whisper and pray in a whisper. That was a prayer-meeting from house to house once or twice—once or twice a week.

"Old Phipps whipped me once. He aimed to kill me but I got loose. He whipped me about a colored girl of his'n that he had by a colored woman.

Phipps went with a colored woman before he married his wife. He had a girl named Martha Ann Phipps. I beat Martha 'bout a pair of stockings. My mistress bought me a nice pair of stockings from the store. You see, they used to knit the stockings. I wore the stockings once; then I washed them and put them on the fence to dry. Martha stole them and put them on. I beat her and took them off of her. She ran and told her father and he ran me home. He couldn't catch me, and he told me he'd get me. I didn't run to my father. I run to my mistress, and he knew he'd better not do nothin' then. He said, 'I'll get you, you little old black somethin'.' Only he didn't say 'somethin'.' He didn't get me then.

"But one day he caught me out by his house. I had gone over that way on an errand I needn't have done. He had two girls hold me. They was Angeline and Nancy. They didn't much want to hold me anyhow. Some niggers would catch you and kill you for the white folks and then there was some that wouldn't. I got loose from them. He tried to hold me hisself but he couldn't. I got away and went back to my old mistress and she wrote him a note never to lay his dirty hands on me again. A little later her brother, Johnson Chatman, came there and ran him off the place. My old mistress' name was Susan Chatman before she married. Then she married Toliver. Then she married Reed. She married Reed last—after Toliver died.

"One old lady named Emily Moorehead runned in and held my mother once for Phipps to whip her. And my mother was down with consumption too. I aimed to git old Phipps for that. But then I got religion and I couldn't do it. Religion makes you forgit a heap of things.

"Susan Reed, my old mistress, bought my father and paid fifteen hundred dollars for him and she hadn't never seen 'im. Advertising. He had run away so much that they had to advertise and sell 'im.

He never would run away from Miss Susan. She was good to him till she got that old nigger beater---Phipps. Her husband, Reed, was called a nigger spoiler. My father was an old man when Phipps was an overseer and wasn't able to fight much then.

"Phipps sure was a bad man. He wasn't so bad neither; but the niggers was scared of him. You know in slave times, sometimes when a master would git too bad, the niggers would kill him---tole him off out in the woods somewheres and git rid of him. Two or three of them would git together and scheme it out, and then two or three of them would git him way out and kill 'im. But they didn't nobody ever pull nothin' like that on Phipps. They was scared of him.

"One time I saw the Yankees a long way off. They had on blue uniforms and was on coal black horses. I hollered out, 'Oh, I see some-thin'.' My mistress said, 'What?' I told her, and she said, 'Them's the Yankees.' She went on in the house and I went with her. She sacked up all the valuables in the house. She said, 'Here,' and she threw a sack of silver on me that was so heavy that I went right on down to the ground. Then she took hold of it and holp me up and holp me carry it out. I carried it out and hid it. She had three buckskin sacks---all full of silver. That wasn't now; that was in slavery times. During the War, Jeff Davis gave out Confederate money. It died out on the folks' hands. About twelve hundred dollars of it died out on my father's hands. But there wasn't nothin' but gold and silver in them sacks.

"I heard them tell the slaves they were free. A man named Captain Barkus who had his arm off at the elbow called for the three near-by plantations to meet at our place. Then he got up on a platform with another man beside him and declared peace and freedom. He p'inted to a colored man and yelled, 'You're free as I am.' Old colored folks, old as I am now, that was on sticks, throwed them sticks away and shouted.

"Right after freedom I stayed with that white woman I told you about. I was with her about four years. I worked for twelve dollars a month and my food and clothes. Then I figured that twelve dollars wasn't enough and I went to work in the field. It was a mighty nice woman. Never hit me in her life. I never have been whipped by a white woman. She was good to me till she died. She died after I had my second child--a girl child.

"I have been living in this city fifteen years. I come from Chicot County when I come here. We came to Arkansas in slavery times. They brought me from Copiah County when I was six or eight years old. When Mrs. Toliver married she came up here and brought my mother. My mother belonged to her son and she said, 'Agnes (that was my mother's name), will you follow me if I buy your husband?' Her husband's name was John Beasley. She said, 'Yes.' Then her old mistress bought Beasley and paid fifteen hundred dollars to get my mother to come with her. Then Peachy went to war and was shot because he come home of a furlough and stayed too long. So when he went back they killed him. My mother nursed him when he was a baby. Old man Toliver said he didn't want none of us to be sold; so they wasn't none of us sold. Maybe there would have been if slavery had lasted longer; but there wasn't.

"Mother really belonged to Peachy, but when Peachy died, then she fell to her mistress.

"I have been a widow now for thirty years. I washed and ironed and plowed and hoed---everything. Now I am gittin' so I ain't able to do nothin' and the Relief keeps me alive. I worked and took care of myself and my last husband and he died, and I ain't married since. I used to take a little boy and make ten bales of cotton. I can't do it now. I used to be a woman in my day. I am my mother's seventh child.

"I don't buy no hoodoo and I don't believe in none, but a seventh child can more or less tell you things that are a long way off. If you want to beat the devil you got to do right. God's got to be in the plan. I tries to do right. I am not perfect but I do the best I can. I ain't got no bottom teeth, but my top ones are good. I have a few bottom ones. The Lawd's keepin' me here for somepin. I been with 'im now seventy-three years."

Interviewer's Comment

I'll bet the grandest moment in the life of Sister Alexander's mother was when her mistress said, "Agnes, will you follow me if I buy your husband?" Fifteen hundred dollars to buy a rebellious slave in order to unite a slave couple. It's epic.

Interviewer_____Miss Irene Robertson_____

Person interviewed_____Ed Allen, Des Arc, Ark.

Age___?___

- -

"I know that after freedom they took care of my pa
and ma and give em a home long as they lived. Ma died wid
young mistress here in Des Arc.

"The present generation is going to the bad. Have
dealings wid em, not good to you. Young folks ain't nice
to you like they used to be.

"White boys and colored boys, whole crowd of us used
to go in the river down here all together, one got in dan-
ger help him out. They don't do it no more. We used to
play base ball together. All had a good time. We never
had to buy a ball or a bat. Always had em. The white boys
bought them. I don't know as who to blame but young folk
changed."

30577

Interviewer   Miss Irene Robertson

Person interviewed Lucindy Allison, Marked Tree, Arkansas
         With children at Biscoe, Arkansas

Age 61

- -

"Ma was a slave in Arkansas. She said she helped grade a hill and help pile up a road between Wicksburg and Wynne. They couldn't put the road over the hill, so they put all the slaves about to grade it down. They don't use the road but it's still there to show for itself.

"She was a tall rawbony woman. Ma was a Hillis and pa's name was Adam Hillis. He learned to trap in slavery and after freedom he followed that for a living. Ma was a sure 'nough field hand. Mama had three sets of children. I don't know how many she did have in all. I had eleven my own self. Grandma was named Tempy and I heard them tell about when she was sold. She and mama went together. They used to whoop the slaves when they didn't work up peart.

"When the 'Old War' come on and the Yankees come they took everything and the black men folks too. They come by right often. They would drive up at mealtime and come in and rake up every blessed thing was cooked. Have to go work scrape about and find something else to eat. What they keer 'bout you being white or black? Thing they was after was filling theirselves up. They done white folks worse than that. They burned their cribs and fences up and their houses too about if they got mad. Things didn't suit them. If they wanted a colored man to go in camp with them and he didn't go, they would shoot you down like a dog. Ma told about some folks she knowd got shot in the yard of his own quarters.

"Us black folks don't want war. They are not war kind of folks. Slavery wasn't right and that 'Old War' wasn't right neither.

"When my children was all little I kept Aunt Mandy Buford till she died. She was a old slave woman. Me and my husband and the biggest children worked in the field. She would sit about and smoke. My boys made cob pipes and cut cane j'ints for 'er to draw through. Red cob pipes was the prettiest. Aunt Mandy said her master would be telling them what to do in the field and he say to her, 'I talking to you too.' She worked right among the men at the same kind of work. She was tall but not large. She carried children on her right hip when she was so young she dragged that foot when she walked. The reason she had to go with the men to the field like she did was 'cause she wasn't no multiplying woman. She never had a chile in all her lifetime. She said her mother nearly got in bad one time when her sister was carrying a baby. She didn't keep up. Said the riding boss got down, dug a hole with the hoe to lay her in it 'cause she was so big in front. Her mother told him if he put her daughter there in that hole she'd cop him up in pieces wid her hoe. He found he had two to conquer and he let her be. But he had to leave 'cause he couldn't whoop the niggers.

"If I could think of all she tole I'd soon have enough to fill up that book you're getting up. I can't recollect who she belong to, and her old talk comes back to me now and then. She talked so much we'd get up and go on off to keep from hearing her tell things over so many times.

"Folks like me what got children think the way they do is all right. I don't like some of my children's ways but none of us perfect. I tells 'em right far as I knows. Times what makes folks no 'count. Times gets stiff around Biscoe. Heap of folks has plenty. Some don't have much--not enough. Some don't have nothing.

"I don't believe in women voting. That ruined the country. We got along very well till they got to tinkering with the government."

Ex-Slave

Amos

Name of Interviewer_____Pernella Anderson_____

Subject_____Early Days in Caledonia - Early days in
                        El Dorado

Ah wuz bo'n de first year niggers wuz free. Wuz born in Cale-
donia at de Primm place. Mah ma belonged tuh George Thompson. After
mah ma died ah stayed wid de Wommacks, a while. Aftuh dat mah pa taken
me home. Pa's name wuz Jesse Flueur. Ah worked lak er slave. Ah out
wood, sawed logs, picked 400 pounds uv cotton evah day. Ah speck ah
married de first time ah wuz about fo'teen years ole. Ah been mahried
three times. All mah husband's is daid. Ole man England and ole
man Cullens run business places and ole man Wooley. His name wuz
reason Wooley. De Woolies got cemetery uv dey own right dar near de
Cobb place. No body is buried in dar but de fambly uv Wooleys. Ole
man Allen Hale he run er store dar too. He is yet livin right dar.
He is real ole. De ole Warren Mitchell place whar ah use tuh live is
Guvment land. Warren Mitchell, he homesteaded the place. We lived
dar and made good crops. De purtiest dar wuz eround, but not hit's
growed up. Don lived dar and made good crops. De purtiest dar wuz
eround. Dar is whah all mah chillun wuz bo'n. Ah use tuh take mah
baby an walk tuh El Dorado to sevice. Ah use tuh come tuh El Dorado
wid a oman by de name of Sue Foster. Nothin but woods when dey laid
de railroad heah. Dey built dem widh hosses and oxes. Ah saw em
when dey whoep de hosses and oxen till dey fall out working dem when
dey laid dat steel. Ah wuz at de first buryin uv de fust pusson buried
in Caledonia graveyard. Huh name wuz Joe Ann Pelk. We set up wid
huh all night and sing and pray. An when we got nearly tuh de church de
bells started tolling and de folks started tuh singin.

When evah any body died dey ring bells tuh let yo know some body
wuz daid. A wuz born on Christmas day, an ah had two chilluns
born on Christmas Day. Dey wuz twins and one uv em had two teeth
and his hair hung down on her shoulders when hit wuz born but hit did
not live but er wek.

Name _____ Josephine Ames _____

Occupation_____ Domestic _____

Resident _____ Ferdville _____

Age____ not given.

Interviewer   Miss Irene Robertson

Person interviewed   Charles Anderson, Helena, Arkansas

Age   77 or 78, not sure

- -

"I was born in Bloomfield, Kentucky. My parents had the same owners.
Mary and Elgin Anderson was their names. They was owned by Isaac Stone.
Davis Stone was their son. They belong to the Stones as far back as they
could remember. Mama was darker than I am. My father was brighter than I
am. He likely had a white father. I never inquired. Mama had colored
parents. Master Stone walked with a big crooked stick. He nor his son
never went to war. Masters in that country never went. Two soldiers were
drafted off our place. I saw the soldiers, plenty of them and plenty times.
There never was no serious happenings.

"The Federal soldiers would come by, sleep in the yard, take our best
horses and leave the broken down ones. Very little money was handled. I
never seen much. Master Stone would give us money like he give money to
Davis. They prized fine stock mostly. They needed money at wheat harvest
time only. When a celebration or circus come through he give us all twenty-
five or thirty cents and told us to go. There wasn't many slaves up there
like down in this country. The owners from all I've heard was crueler and
sold them off oftener here.

"Weaving was a thing the women prided in doing--being a fast weaver or
a fine hand at weaving. They wove pretty coverlets for the beds. I see
colored spreads now makes me think about my baby days in Kentucky.

"Freedom was something mysterious. Colored folks didn't talk it. White folks didn't talk it. The first I realized something different, Master Stone was going to whip a older brother. He told mama something I was too small to know. She said, 'Don't leave this year, son. I'm going to leave.' Master didn't whip him.

"Master Stone's cousin kept house for him. I remember her well. They were all very nice to us always. He had a large farm. He had twenty servants in his yard. We all lived there close together. My sister and mama cooked. We had plenty to eat. We had beef in spring and summer. Mutton and kid on special occasions. We had hog in the fall and winter. We had geese, ducks, and chickens. We had them when we needed them. We had a field garden. He raised corn, wheat, oats, rye, and tobacco.

"Once a year we got dressed up. We got shirts, a suit, pants and shoes, and what else we needed to wear. Then he told them to take care of their clothes. They got plenty to do a year. We didn't have fine clothes no time. We didn't eat ham and chicken. I never seen biscuit--only some-times.

"I seen a woman sold. They had on her a short dress, no sleeves, so they could see her muscles, I reckon. They would buy them and put them with good healthy men to raise young slaves. I heard that. I was very small when I seen that young woman sold and years later I heard that was what was done.

"I don't know when freedom come on. I never did know. We was five or six years breaking up. Master Stone never forced any of us to leave. He give some of them a horse when they left. I cried a year to go back. It was a dear place to me and the memories linger with me every day.

"There was no secret society or order of Ku Klux in reach of us as I ever heard.

"I voted Republican ticket. We would go to Jackson to vote. There would be a crowd. The last I voted was for Theodore Roosevelt. I voted here in Helena for years. I was on the petit jury for several years here in Helena.

"I farmed in your state some (Arkansas). I farmed all my young life. I been in Arkansas sixty years. I come here February 1879 with distant relatives. They come south. When I come to Helena there was but one set of mechanics. I started to work. I learned to paint and hang wall paper. I've worked in nearly every house in Helena.

"The present times are gloomy. I tried to prepare for old age. I had a apartment house and lost it. I owned a home and lost it. They foreclosed me out.

"The present generation is not doing as well as I have.

"My health knocked me out. My limbs swell, they are stiff. I have a bad bladder trouble.

"I asked for help but never have got none. If I could got a little relief I never would lost my house. They work my wife to death keeping us from starving. She sewed till they cut off all but white ladies. When she got sixty-five they let her go and she got a little job cooking. They never give us no relief."

Interviewer_____Miss Irene Robertson

Person interviewed_____Nancy Anderson
                                 Street H, West Memphis, Arkansas
Age   66

- -

"I was born at Sanitobia, Mississippi. Mother died when I was a child.
I was three months old, they said, when I lost her. Father lived to be very
old. My mother was Ella Geeter and my stepmother was Lucy Evans. My
father's name was Si Hubbard. My parents married after the War. I
remembers Grandma Harriett Hubbard. She said she was sold. She was a
cook and she raised my papa up with white folks. Her children was sold with
her. Papa was sold too at the same time. Papa fired a steam gin. They
ground corn and ginned cotton.

"I stayed with Sam Hall's family. She was good to me. I had a small
bed by the fireplace. She kept me with two of her own children. Some of
the girls and boys I was raised up with live at Sanitobia now and have fine
homes. When we would be playing they would take all the toys from me. Miss
Fannie would say, 'Poor Nancy ain't got no toys.' Then they would put them
on the floor and we would all play. They had a little table. We all eat at
it. We had our own plates. We all eat out of tin plates and had tin cups.

"They couldn't keep me at home when papa married. I slipped off across
the pasture. There was cows and hogs in there all the time. I wasn't
afraid of them. I would get behind Miss Fannie and hide in her dress tail
when they come after me. They let me stay most of the time for about five
years. Sam Hall was good to my father and Miss Fannie about raised me after
my mother died. She made me mind but she was good to me.

"Grandma lived with papa. She was part Indian. As long as papa lived he share cropped and ginned. He worked as long as he was able to hit a lick. He died four miles east out from Sanitobia on Mr. Hayshaws place. What I told you is what I know. He said he was sold that one time. Hubbards had plenty to eat and wear. He was a boy and they didn't want to stunt the children. Papa was a water boy and filed the hoes for the chopping hands. He carried a file along with them hoeing and would sharpen their hoes and fetch 'em water in their jugs. Aunt Sallie, his sister, took keer of the children.

"Papa went to the War. He could blow his bugle and give all the war signals. He got the military training. Him and his friend Charlie Grim used to step around and show us how they had to march to orders. His bugle had four joints. I don't know what went with it. From what they said they didn't like the War and was so glad to get home.

"Between the big farms they had worm fences (rail fences) and gates. You had to get a pass from your master to go visiting. The gates had big chains and locks on them. Some places was tollgates where they traveled over some man's land to town. On them roads the man owned the place charged. He kept some boy to open and shut the gate. They said the gates was tall.

"Some of the slaves that had hard masters run off and stay in the woods. They had nigger dogs and would run them--catch 'em. He said one man (Negro) was hollowing down back of the worm fence close to where they was working. They all run to him. A great long coachwhip snake was wrapped 'round him, his arms and all, and whooping him with its tail. It cut gashes like a knife and the blood poured. The overseer cut

the snake's head off with his big knife and they carried him home bleeding.
His master didn't whoop him, said he had no business off in the woods. He
had run off. His master rubbed salt in the gashes. It nearly killed him.
It burnt him so bad. That stopped the blood. They said sut (soot) would
stopped the blood but it would left black mark. The salt left white marks
on him. The salt helped kill the pison (poison). Some masters and over-
seers was cruel. When they was so bad marked they didn't bring a good
price. They thought they was hard to handle.

"Aunt Jane Peterson, old friend of mine, come to visit me nearly every
year after she got so old. She told me things took place in slavery times.
She was in Virginia till after freedom. She had two girls and a boy with a
white daddy. She told me all about how that come. She said no chance to
run off or ever get off, you had to stay and take what come. She never got
to marry till after freedom. Then she had three more black children by her
husband. She said she was the cook. Old master say, 'Jane, go to the lot
and get the eggs.' She was scared to go and scared not to go. He'd beat
her out there, put her head between the slip gap where they let the hogs
into the pasture from the lot down back of the barn. She say, 'Old missis
whip me. This ain't right.' He'd laugh. Said she bore three of his
children in a room in the same house his family lived in. She lived in
the same house. She had a room so as she could build fires and cook break-
fast by four o'clock sometimes, she said. She was so glad freedom come on
and soon as she heard it she took her children and was gone, she said.
She had no use for him. She was scared to death of him. She learned to
pray and prayed for freedom. She died in Cold Water, Mississippi. She was
so glad freedom come on before her children come on old enough to sell.

Part white children sold for more than black children. They used them for

house girls.

"I don't know Ku Klux stories enough to tell one. These old tales leave my mind. I'm 66 and all that was before my time.

"Times is strange--hard, too. But the way I have heard they had to work and do and go I hardly ever do grumble. I've heard so much. I got children and I do the best I can by them. That is all I can do or say."

Interviewer   Samuel S. Taylor

Person interviewed   R. B. Anderson
          Route 4, Box 68 (near Granite)
Age 76   Little Rock, Arkansas

- - - - - - - - - [The Brooks-Baxter War] - - - - -

"I was born in Little Rock along about Seventeenth and Arch Streets.
There was a big plantation there then. Dr. Wright owned the plantation.
He owned my mother and father. My father and mother told me that I was born
in 1862. They didn't know the date exactly, so I put it the last day in the
year and call it December 30, 1862.

"My father's name was William Anderson. He didn't go to the War
because he was blind. He was ignorant too. He was colored. He was a
pretty good old man when he died.

"My mother's name was Minerva Anderson. She was three-fourths Indian,
hair way down to her waist. I was in Hot Springs blacking boots when my
mother died. I was only about eight or ten years old then. I always
regretted I wasn't able to do anything for my mother before she died. I
don't know to what tribe her people belonged.

"Dr. Wright was awful good to his slaves.

"I don't know just how freedom came to my folks. I never heard my
father say. They were set free, I know. They were set free when the War
ended. They never bought their freedom.

"We lived on Tenth and near to Center in a one-room log house.
That is the earliest thing I remember. When they moved from there, my
father had accumulated enough to buy a home. He bought it at Seventh
and Broadway. He paid cash for it--five hundred and fifty dollars.

That is where we all lived until it was sold. I couldn't name the date of the sale but it was sold for good money—about three thousand eight hundred dollars, or maybe around four thousand. I was a young man then.

"I remember the Brooks-Baxter War.
"I remember the King White fooled a lot of niggers and armed them and brought them up here. The niggers and Republicans here fought them and run them back where they come from.
"I know Hot Springs when the main street was a creek. I can't remember when I first went there. The government bath-house was called 'Ral Hole', because it was mostly people with bad diseases that went there.
"After the War, my father worked for a rich man named Hunter. He was yardman and took care of the horse. My mother was living then.
"Scipio Jones and I were boys together. We slept on pool tables many a time when we didn't have no other place to sleep. He was poor when he was a boy and glad to get hold of a dime, or a nickel. He and I don't speak today because he robbed me. I had a third interest in my place. I gave him money to buy my place in for me. It was up for sale and I wanted to get posses- sion. He gave me some papers to sign and when I found out what was happening, he had all my property. My wife kept me from killing him."

Interviewer's Comment
Occupation: Grocer, bartender, porter, general work

30033

Interviewer   Mrs. Bernice Bowden

Person interviewed   Sarah Anderson
                      3815 W. Second Avenue, Pine Bluff, Arkansas
Age   78?

- -

"I don't know when I was born. When the Civil War ended, I was bout four or five years old.

"I jes' remember when the people come back---the soldiers---when the War ended. We chillun run under the house. That was the Yankees.

"I was born in Bibb County, Georgia. That's where I was bred and born.

"I been in Arkansas ever since I was fourteen. That was shortly after the Civil War, I reckon. We come here when they was emigratin' to Arkansas. I'm tellin' you the truth, I been here a long time.

"I member when the soldiers went by and we chillun run under the house. It was the Yankee cavalry, and they made so much noise. Dat's what the old folks told us. I member dat we run under the house and called ourself hidin'.

"My master was Madison Newsome and my missis was Sarah Newsome. Named after her? Must a done it. Me and her chillun was out wallowin' in the dirt when the Yankees come by. Sometimes I stayed in the house with my white folks all night.

"My mother and father say they was well treated. That's what they say.

"Old folks didn't low us chillun round when they was talkin' bout their business, no ma'am.

"We stayed with old master a good while after freedom---till they commenced emigratin' from Georgia to Arkansas. Yes ma'am!

"I'm the mother of fourteen chillun--two pairs of twins. I married young--bout fifteen or sixteen, I reckon. I married a young fellow. I say we was just chaps. After he died, I married a old settled man and now he's dead.

"I been livin' a pretty good life. Seems like the white folks just didn't want me to get away from their chillun.

"All my chillun dead cept one son. He was a twin."

Interviewer_____Miss Irene Robertson_____

Person interviewed___Selie Anderson, Holly Grove, Arkansas___

Age___78___

- -

"I was born near Decatur, Alabama and lived there till I was fifteen
years old. Course I members hearin' em talk bout Mars Newt. I named fur
my ma's old mistress -- Miss Selie Thompson and Mars Newt Thompson. Pa
died when I was three years old. He was a soldier. Ma had seven child-
ren. They have bigger families then than they have now. Ma name
Emmaline Thompson. Pa name Sam Adair. I can't tell you about him. I
heard em say his pa was a white man. He was light skinned. Old folks
didn't talk much foe children so I don't know well nough to tell you bout
him. Ma was a cook and a licensed midwife in Alabama. She waited on both
black and white. Ma never staid at home much. She worked out. I come to
Mississippi after I married and had one child. Ma and all come. Ma went
to Tom McGehee's to cook after freedom. She married old man named Lewis
Chase and they worked on where he had been raised. His name was Lewis
Sprangle. He looked after the stock and drove the carriage. Daniel
Sprangle had a store and a big farm. He had three girls and three boys.
I was their house girl. Mama lived on the place and give me to em cause
they could do better part by me than she could. I was six years old when
she give me to em. They lernt me to sweep, knit, crochet, piece quilts.
She lernt her children thater way sometimes. Miss Nancy Sprangle didn't
treat me no different from her own girls. Miss Dora married Mr. Pitt Loney

and I was dressed up and held up her train (long dress and veil). I
stayed with Miss Dora after she married. One of the girls married Mr.
John Galbreth. I married and went home then come to Mississippi. Mrs.
Gables, Mr. Gables was old people but they had two adopted boys. I took
them boys to the field to work wid my children. She sewed for me and my
children. Her girls cooked all we et in busy times. They done work at
the house but they didn't work in the field.

"I been married five times. Every time I married I married at home.
Mighty little marryin' goin' on now — mighty little. Mama stayed wid Mr.
Sprangle till we all got grown. Miss Nancy's girls married so that all
the way I knowd how to do. I had a good time. I danced every chance I
got. I been well blessed all my life till I'm gettin' feeble now.

"Papa run the gin on Mr. Sprangle's place, then he went to war, come
back foe he died. I recken he come home sick cause he died pretty soon.

"I jess can member this Ku Klux broke down our door wid hatchets. It
scared us all to death. They didn't do nuthin' to us. They was huntin'
Uncle Jeff. He wasn't bout our house. He was ox driver fer Mr. Sprangle.
Him and a family of pore white folks got to fussin' bout a bridle. Some
of em was dressed up when they come to our house ma said. After that Mr.
Kirby killed him close to his home startin' out one mornin' to work. His
name was Uncle Jeff Saxon. Ma knowd it was some of the men right on Mr.
Sprangle's place whut come to our house.

"I live wid my daughter. I get $8 from the Welfare.

"If they vote for better it be all right. I never seen no poles. I
don't know how they vote. I'm too old to start up votin'.

"Lawd you got me now. The times changed and got so fast. It all beyond me. I jes' listens. I don't know whut goner happen to this young generation."

Interviewer _____ Samuel S. Taylor _____

Person interviewed _____ W. A. Anderson (dark brown) _____
                         3200 W. 18th Street, Little Rock, Arkansas

Age __78__

     Occupation _____ House and yard man _____

- - - - - - - - - - - [Serves the "Lawd"] - - - - - - - - -

"I don't know nothin' about slavery. You know I wouldn't know nothin' bout it cause I was only four years old when the war ended. All I know is I was born in slavery; but I don't know nothin' bout it.

"I don't remember nothin' of my parents. Times was all confused and old folks didn't talk before chilun. They didn't have time. Besides, my mother and father were separated.

"I was born in Arkansas and have lived here all my life. But I don't gossip and entertain. I just moved in this house last week. Took a wheel-barrow and brought all these things here myself.

"Those boys out there jus' threw a stone against the house. I thought the house was falling. I work all day and when night comes, I'm tired.

"I don't have no wife, no children, nothin'; nobody to help me out. I don't ask the neighbors nothin' cept to clear out this junk they left here.

"I ain't goin' to talk about the Ku Klux. I got other things to think about. It takes all my time and strength to do my work and live a Christian. Folks got so nowadays they don't care bout nothin'. I just live here and serve the Lawd."

Interviewer's Comments

Anderson is separated from his wife who left him. He lost his home a short time ago. A few months ago, he was so sick he was expected to die. He supports himself through the friendliness of a few white people who give him odds and ends of work to do.

I made three calls on him, helped him set up his stoves and his beds and clear up his house a little bit since he had just moved into it and had a good deal of work to do. His misfortunes have made him unwilling to talk just now, but he will give a good interview later I am certain.

Interviewer   Miss Irene Robertson

Person interviewed Henry Anthony; R.F.D. #1, Biscoe, Arkansas

Age   84

- -

"I was born at Jackson, North Carolina. My master and mistress
named Betsy and Jason Williams but my pa's name was Anthony. My young
master was a orderly seargent. He took me wid him to return some mules
and wagons. He showed me what he want done an I followed him round wid
wagons. The wagons hauled ammnition and provisions. Pa worked for the
master and ma cooked. They got sold to Lausen Capert. When freedom
come they went back and stayed a month or two at Williams then we all
went back to John Odom. We stayed round close and farmed and worked
till they died. I married and when I had four or five children I heard
ob dis country. I come on immigration ticket to Mr. Aydelott here at
Biscoe. Train full of us got together and come. One white man got us
all up and brought us here to Biscoe. I farmed for Mr. Aydelott four
or five years, then for Mr. Bland, Mr. Scroggin.

"I never went to school a day in my life. I used to vote here in
Biscoe right smart. I let the young folks do my votin. They can tell
more about it. I sho do not think it is the woman's place to vote an
hold all the jobs from the men. Iffen you don't in the Primary cause
you don't know nuf to pick out a man, you sho don't know nuthin er tall
bout votin in the General lection. In fact it ain't no good to our
race nohow.

"The whole world gone pass my judgment long ago. I jess sets round to see what they say an do next. It is bad when you caint get work you able to do an that's hard on the old folks. I could saved. I did save right smart. Sickness come on. Sometimes you have a bad crop year, make nuthin, but you have to live on. Young folks don't see no hard times if they keep well an able to work.

"I get commodities and $6 a month. I do a little if I can.

One time my son bought a place fo me and him. He paid all cept $70. I don't know whut it cost now. It was 47 acres. I worked on it three years. He sold it and went to the sawmill. He say he come out square on it. I didn't wanter sell it but he did."

Interviewer   Mrs. Bernice Bowden

Person interviewed   Katie Arbery
         815 W. Thirteenth, Pine Bluff, Arkansas

Age 80

- -

"I am eighty years old. My name 'fore I was a Arbery was Baxter. My mother was a Baxter. Born in Union County.

"My mother's first people was Baxter and my grandmother was a Baxter and they just went by that name; she never did change her name.

"The boss man--that was what they called our master--his name was Paul McCall. He was married twice. His oldest son was Jim McCall. He was in the War. Yes ma'am, the Civil War.

"Paul McCall raised me up with his chillun and I never did call him master, just called him pappy, and Jim McCall, I called him brother Jim. Just raised us all up there in the yard. My grandmother was the cook.

"There wasn't no fightin' in Union County but I 'member when the Yankees was goin' through and singin'

> 'The Union forever, hurrah, boys, hurrah
> We'll rally 'round the flag, boys,
> Shouting the battle cry of freedom.'

(She sang this--ed.)

And I 'member this one good:

> 'Old buckwheat cakes and good strong butter
> To make your lips go flip, flip, flutter,
> Look away, look away, look away, Dixie land.'

"Pappy used to play that on his fiddle and have us chillun tryin' to dance. Used to call us chillun and say, 'You little devils, come up here and dance' and have us marchin'.

"My cousin used to be a quill blower. Brother Jim would out fishin'
canes and plat 'em together--they called 'em a pack--five in a row, just like
my fingers. Anybody that knowed how could sure make music on 'em. Tom
Rollins, that was my baby uncle, he was a banjo picker.

"I can remember a heap a things that happened, but 'bout slavery, I
didn't know one day from another. They treated us so nice that when they
said freedom come, I thought I was always free.

"I heered my grandmother talk about sellin' 'em, but I was just a
little kid and I didn't know what they was talkin' about. I heered 'em say,
'Did you know they sold Aunt Sally away from her baby?' I heered 'em talkin',
I know that much.

"After freedom, our folks stayed right on Paul McCall's place. My
grandmother cooked for the McCalls till I was eight or nine years old, then
she cooked for the McCrays--they was all relatives--till I was twenty-one.
Then I married.

"Paul McCall first married in the Baxter family and then he married into
the McCray family. I lived on the McCall place till I was grown. They all
come from Alabama. Yes'm, they come befo' the war was.

"Chillun in dem days paid attention. People raised chillun in dem days.
Folks just feeds 'em now and lets 'em grow up.

"I looks at the young race now and they is as wise as rabbits.

"I never went to school but three months, but I never will forget that
old blue back McGuffey's. Sam Porter was our teacher and I was scared of
him. I was so scared I couldn't learn nothin'.

"As far as I can remember I have been treated nice everywhere I been.
Ain't none of the white folks ever mistreated me.

"Lord, we had plenty to eat in slavery days---and freedom days too.

"One time when my mother was cookin' for Colonel Morgan and my oldest brother was workin' some land, my mother always sent me over with a bucket of milk for him. So one day she say, 'Snooky, come carry your brother's milk and hurry so he can have it for dinner.' I was goin' across a field that was a awful deer country. I had on a red dress and was goin' on with my milk when I saw a old buck lookin' at me. All at once he went 'whu-u-u', and then the whole drove came up. There was mosely trees (I think she must have meant mimosa---ed.) in the field and I run and climbed up in one of 'em. A mosely tree grows crooked; I don't care how straight you put it in the ground, it's goin' to grow crooked. So I climb up in the mosely tree and begin to yell. My brother heard me and come 'cause he knowed what was up. He used to say, 'Now, Snipe, when you come 'cross that mosely field, don't you wear that old red dress 'cause they'll get you down and tear that dress off you.' I liked the dress 'cause he had give it to me. I had set the milk down at the foot of the tree and it's a wonder they didn't knock it over, but when my brother heard me yell he come a runnin' with a gun and shot one of the deer. I got some of the venison and he give some to Colonel Morgan, his boss man. Colonel Morgan had fought in the war.

"The reason I can't tell you no more is, since I got old my mind goes this and that a way.

"But I can tell you all the doctors that doctored on me. They give me up to die once. I had the chills from the first of one January to the next. We had Dr. Chester and Dr. McCray and Dr. Lewis---his name was Perry---and Dr. Green and Dr. Smead. Took quinine till I couldn't hear, and finally Dr. Green said, 'We'll just quit givin' her medicine, looks like she's goin' to die anyway.'

And then Dr. Lewis fed me for three weeks steady on okra soup cooked with chicken. Just give me the broth. Then I commenced gettin' better and here I am.

"But I can't work like I used to. When I was young I could work right along with the men but I can't do it now. I wish I could 'cause they's a heap a things I'd like that my chillun and grandchillun can't get for me.

"Well, good-bye, come back again sometime."

30598

Interviewer_____ Samuel S. Taylor _____

Person interviewed_____ Campbell Armstrong _____
                          802 Schiller Street, Little Rock, Arkansas

Age __86__

[Boys Liked Corn Shuckings]

"I couldn't tell you when I was born. I was born a good while before
freedom. I was a boy about ten years old in the time of the Civil War.
That would make me about eighty-five or six years old.

"My father's name was Cy Armstrong. My mother's name was Gracie Arm-
strong. I don't know the names of my grandparents. They was gone when I
got here. My sister died right there in the corner of the next room.

House and Furniture

"I used to live in an old log house. Take dirt and dob the cracks.
The floors were these here planks. We had two windows and one door. That
was in Georgia, in Houston County, on old Dempsey Brown's place. I know
him--know who dug his grave.

"They had beds nailed up to the side of the house. People had a
terrible time you know. White folks had it all. When I come along they
had it and they had it ever since I been here. You didn't have no chance
like folks have nowadays. Just made benches and stools to sit on. Made
tables out of planks. I never saw any cupboards and things like that. Them
things wasn't thought about then. The house was like a stable then. But
them log houses was better than these 'cause the wind couldn't get through
them.

Work as a Boy

"I wasn't doin' nothin' but totin' water. I toted water for a whole year when I was a boy about eight years old. I was the water boy for the field hands. Later I worked out in the fields myself. They would make me sit on my mammy's row to help keep her up.

Free Negroes

"You better not say you were free them days. If you did, they'd tell you to get out of there. You better not stop on this side of the Mason Dixie Line either. You better stop on the other side. Whenever a nigger got so he couldn't mind, they'd take him down and whip him. They'd whip the free niggers just the same as they did the slaves.

Marriage

"You see that broom there? They just lay that broom down and step over it. That was all the marriage they knowed about.

Corn Shuckings

"The boys used to just get down and raise a holler and shuck that corn. Man, they had fun! They sure liked to go to those corn shuckings. They danced and went on. They'd give 'em whiskey too. That's all I know about it.

Rations

"They'd weigh the stuff out and give it to you and you better not go back. They'd give you three pounds of meat and a quart of meal and molasses when they'd make it. Sometimes they would take a notion to give you something like flour. But you had to take what they give you. They give out the rations every Saturday. That was to last you a week.

Patrollers

"I was at a ball one night. They had fence rails in the fire.
Patroller knocked at the door, stepped in and closed it behind him. Nigger
pulled a rail out of the fire and stuck it 'gainst the patroller and that
patroller stepped aside and let that nigger get by. Niggers used to tie
ropes across the road so that the patrollers' horses would trip up.

Mulattoes

"I never seed any mulattoes then. That thing is something that just
come up. Old Dempsey Brown, if he seed a white man goin' 'round with the
nigger women on his place, he run him away from there. But that's gwine on
in the full now.

"That ought not to be. If God had wanted them people to mix, he'd have
mixed 'em. God made 'em red and white and black. And I'm goin' to stay
black. I ain't climbed the fence yet and I won't climb it now. I don't
know. I don't believe in that. If you are white be white, and if you are
black be black. Children need to go out and play but these boys ought not
to be 'lowed to run after these girls.

Whippings

"Your overseer carried their straps with them. They had 'em with 'em
all the time. Just like them white folks do down to the County Farm. Used
to use a man just like he was a beast. They'd make him lay down on the
ground and whip him. They'd had to shoot me down. That is the reason I
tend to my business. If he wouldn't lay down they'd call for help and strap
him down and stretch him out. Put one man on one arm and another on the
other. They'd pull his clothes down and whip the blood out of him. Them
people didn't care what they done since they didn't do right.

Freedom

"When I first heard them talking about freedom, I didn't know what freedom was. I was there standin' right up and looking at 'em when they told us we was free. And master said, 'You all free now. You can go where you want to.'

"They never give you a thing when they freed you. They give you some work to do. They never looked for nothin' only to go to work. The white folks always had the best of it.

"When Abe Lincoln first freed 'em, they all stood together. If this one was ill the others went over and sit up with him. If he needed something they'd carry it to him. They don't do that now. They done well then. As soon as they quit standing together then they had trouble.

Wages Then

"Fellow said to me, 'Campbell, I want you to split up them blocks and pile 'em up for me.' I said, 'What you goin' to pay me?' He said, 'I'll pay you what is right.' I said, 'That won't do; you have to tell me what you goin' to give me before I start to work.' And he said to me, 'You can git to hell out of here.'

Selling and Buying Slaves

"They'd put you up on the block and sell you. That is just what they'd do--sell you. These white folks will do anything,--anything they want to do. They'd take your clothes off just like you was some kind of a beast.

"You used to be worth a thousand dollars then, but you're not worth two bits now. You ain't worth nothin' when you're free.

Refugees -- Jeff Davis

"They used to come to my place in droves. Wagons would start coming in in the morning and they wouldn't stop coming in till two or three in the evening. They'd just be travelin' to keep out the way of the Yankees. They caught old Jeff Davis over in Twiggs County. That's in Georgia. Caught him in Buzzard's Roost. That was only about four or five miles from where I was. I was right down yonder in Houston County. Twigg County and Houston County is adjoinin'. I never saw any of the soldiers but they was following them though.

Voters

"I have seen plenty of niggers voting. I wasn't old enough to vote in Georgia. I come in Arkansas and I found out how the folks used themselves and I come out that business. They was selling themselves just like cattle and I wouldn't have nothing to do with that.

"I knew Jerry Lawson, who was Justice of Peace. He was a nigger, a low-down devil. Man, them niggers done more dirt in this city. The Republicans had this city and state. I went to the polls and there was very few white folks there. I knew several of them niggers--Mack Armstrong, he was Justice of Peace. I can't call the rest of them. Nothing but old thieves. If they had been people, they'd been honest. Wouldn't sell their brother. It is bad yet. They still stealin' yet.

Ku Klux

"That's another devil. Man, I'll tell you we seen terrible times. I don't know nothing much about 'em myself. I know one thing. Abe Lincoln said, 'Kill him wherever you see him.'

Self-Support and Support of Aged Slaves
in Slave Times

"A white man asked me how much they givin' me. I said, 'Eight dollars.' He said, 'You ought to be gittin' twenty-five.' I said, 'Maybe I ought to be but I ain't.'

"I ain't able to do no work now. I ain't able to tote that wood hardly. I don't git as much consideration as they give the slaves back yonder. They didn't make the old people in slavery work when they was my age. My daddy when he was my age, they turned him out. They give him a rice patch where he could make his rice. When he died, he had a whole lot of rice. They stopped putting all the slaves out at hard labor when they got old. That's one thing. White folks will take care of their old ones. Our folks won't do it. They'll take a stick and kill you. They don't recognize you're human. Their parents don't teach them. Folks done quit teaching their children. They don't teach them the right thing no more. If they don't do, then they ought to make them do.

Little Rock

"I been here about twenty years in Little Rock. I went and bought this place and paid for it. Somebody stole seventy-five dollars from me right here in this house. And that got me down. I ain't never been able to git up since.

"I paid a man for what he did for me. He said, 'Well, you owe me fifteen cents.' When he got done he said, 'You owe me fifty cents.' You can't trust a man in the city.

"I was living down in England. That's a little old country town. I come here to Little Rock where I could be in a city. I done well. I bought this place.

"I reckon I lived in Arkansas about thirty years before I left and come here to Little Rock. When I left Georgia, I come to Arkansas and settled down in Lonoke County, made crops there. I couldn't tell you how long I stayed there. I didn't keep no record of it at all. I come out of Lonoke County and went into Jefferson.

"Man, I was never in such shape as I am in now. That devilish stock law killed me. It killed all the people. Nobody ain't been able to do nothin' since they passed the stock law. I had seventy-five hogs and twenty cows. They made a law you had to keep them chickens up, keep them hogs up, keep them cows up. They shoots at every right thing, and the wrong things they don't shoot at. God don't uphold no man to set you up in the jail when you ain't done nothin'. You didn't have no privilege then (slave time), and you ain't got none now."

Interviewer
Pernella Anderson, colored.

30012

El Dorado Division
Federal Writers' Project
Union County, Arkansas

75

EX-SLAVE AND RIDDLES

"I was born in the Junction city community and belonged to the Cooks. I was ten years old at surrender. Mother and father had 12 children and we lived in a one room log cabin and cooked on a fireplace and oven. Mos and Miss Cook did not allow ma and pa to whip me. When ever I do something and I knew I was going to get a whipping I would make it to old Miss. She would keep me from getting that whipping. I was a devilish boy. I would do everything in the world I could think of just for devilment. Old mos was sure good to his slaves. I never went to school a day in my life. Old Miss would carry me to church sometimes when it was hot so we could fan for her. We used palmeter fan leaves for fans. We ate pretty good in slavery time, but we did not have all of this late stuff. Some of our dishes was possum stew, vegetables, persimmon pie and tato bread. Ma did not allow us to sit around grown folks. When they were talking she always made us get under the bed. Our bed was made from pine poles. We children slept on pallets on the floor. The way slaves married in slavery time they jumped over the broom and when they separated they jumped backward over the broom. Times were better in slavery time to my notion than they are now because they did not go hungry, neither necked. They ate common and wore one kind of clothes."

A duck, a bullfrog and a skunk went to a circus. the duck and the bullfrog got in, why didn't the skunk get in?.
(Answer). The duck had a bill, the bullfrog had a greenback but the skunk had nothing but a scent.

If your father's sister is not your aunt what kin is she to you? (your mother).

What is the difference between a four quart measure and a side saddle?
(Answer). They both hold a gallon. (a gal on)

-Cora Armstrong, colored.

30902

Interviewer _____ Miss Irene Robertson _____

Person interviewed_____ Lillie Baccus, Madison, Arkansas _____

Age __73 __

- -

"I'll tell you what I heard. I was too little to remember the Civil
War. Mama's owner was _____ Dillard. She called him 'Master' Dillard.
Papa's owner was _____ Smith. He called him 'Master' Smith. Mama was
named Ann and papa Arthur Smith. I was born at West Point, Mississippi. I
heard ma say she was sold. She said Pattick sold her. She had to leave
her two children Cherry and Ann. Mama was a field hand. So was grandma
yet she worked in the house some she said. After freedom Cherry and Ann
come to mama. She was going to be sold agin but was freed before sold.

"Mama didn't live only till I was about three years old, so I don't
know enough to tell you about her. Grandma raised us. She was sold twice.
She said she run out of the house to pick up a star when the stars fell.
They showered down and disappeared.

"The Yankees camped close to where they lived, close to West Point,
Mississippi, but in the country close to an artesian well. The well was on
their place. The Yankees stole grandma and kept her at their tent. They
meant to take her on to wait on them and use but when they started to move
old master spicioned they had her hid down there. He watched out and seen
her when they was going to load her up. He went and got the head man to make them
give her up. She was so glad to come home. Glad to see him cause she
wanted to see him. They watched her so close she was afraid they would
shoot her leaving. She lived to be 101 years old. She raised me.

She used to tell how the overseer would whip her in the field. They
wasn't good to her in that way.

"I have three living children and eleven dead. I married twice. My
first husband is living. My second husband is dead. I married in day
time in the church the last time. All else ever took place in my life was
hard work. I worked in the field till I was too old to hit a tap. I live
wid my children. I get $8 and commodities.

"I come to Arkansas because they said money was easy to get—growed on
bushes. I had four little children to make a living for and they said it
was easier.

"I think people is better than they was long time ago. Times is
harder. People have to buy everything they have as high as they is, makes
money scarce nearly bout a place as hen's teeth. Hens ain't got no teeth.
We don't have much money I tell you. The Welfare gives me $8."

Interviewer_____ Samuel S. Taylor_____

Person interviewed_____ Joseph Samuel Badgett_____
                                   1221 Wright Avenue, Little Rock, Arkansas

Age___72___

[Mother Was a Fighter]

"My mother had Indian in her. She would fight. She was the pet of
the people. When she was out, the pateroles would whip her because she
didn't have a pass. She has showed me scars that were on her even till the
day that she died. She was whipped because she was out without a pass.
She could have had a pass any time for the asking, but she was too proud to
ask. She never wanted to do things by permission.

Birth

"I was born in 1864. I was born right here in Dallas County. Some of
the most prominent people in this state came from there. I was born on
Thursday, in the morning at three o'clock, May the twelfth. My mother has
told me that so often, I have it memorized.

Persistence of Slave Customs

"While I was a slave and was born close to the end of the Civil War,
I remember seeing many of the soldiers down here. I remember much of the
treatment given to the slaves. I used to say 'master' myself in my day. We
had to do that till after '69 or '70. I remember the time when I couldn't
go nowhere without asking the 'white folks.' I wasn't a slave then but I
couldn't go off without asking the white people. I didn't know no better.

"I have known the time in the southern part of this state when if
you wanted to give an entertainment you would have to ask the white folks.

Didn't know no better. For years and years, most of the niggers just stayed with the white folks. Didn't want to leave them. Just took what they give 'em and didn't ask for nothing different.

"If I had known forty years ago what I know now!

First Negro Doctor in Tulip, Arkansas

"The first Negro doctor we ever seen come from Little Rock down to Tulip, Arkansas. We were all excited. There were plenty of people who didn't have a doctor living with twenty miles of them. When I was fourteen years old, I was secretary of a conference.

Schooling

"What little I know, an old white woman taught me. I started to school under this old woman because there weren't any colored teachers. There wasn't any school at Tulip where I lived. This old lady just wanted to help. I went to her about seven years. She taught us a little every year—'specially in the summer time. She was high class—a high class Christian woman—belonged to the Presbyterian church. Her name was Mrs. Gentry Wiley.

"I went to school to Scipio Jones once. Then they opened a public school at Tulip and J. C. Smith taught there two years in the summer time. Then Lula Baily taught there one year. She didn't know no more than I did. Then Scipio came. He was there for a while. I don't remember just how long.

"After that I went to Pine Bluff. The County Judge at that time had the right to name a student from each district. I was appointed and went up there in '82 and '83 from my district. It took about eight years to finish Branch Normal at that time. I stayed there two years. I roomed with old man John Young.

"You couldn't go to school without paying unless you were sent by the Board. We lived in the country and I would go home in the winter and study in the summer. Professor J. C. Corbin was principal of the Pine Bluff Branch Normal at that time. Dr. A. H. Hill, Professor Booker, and quite a number of the people we consider distinguished were in school then. They finished, but I didn't. I had to go to my mother because she was ill. I don't claim to have no schooling at all.

"Forty Acres and a Mule"

"My mother received forty acres of land when freedom came. Her master gave it to her. She was given forty acres of land and a colt. There is no more to tell about that. It was just that way--a gift of forty acres of land and a colt from her former master.

"My mother died. There is a woman living now that lost it (the home). Mother let Malinda live on it. Mother lived with the white folks meanwhile. She didn't need the property for herself. She kept it for us. She built a nice log house on it. Fifteen acres of it was under cultivation when it was given to her. My sister lived on it for a long time. She mortgaged it in some way I don't know how. I remember when the white people ran me down there some years back to get me to sign a title to it. I didn't have to sign the paper because the property had been deeded to Susan Badgett and HEIRS; lawyers advised me not to sign it. But I signed it for the sake of my sister.

Father and Master

"My mother's master was named Badgett--Captain John Badgett. He was a Methodist preacher. Some of the Badgetts still own property on Main Street. My mother's master's father was my daddy.

Marriage

"I was married July 12, 1889. Next year I will have been married fifty years. My wife's name was Elizabeth Owens. She was born in Batesville, Mississippi. I met her at Brinkley when she was visiting her aunt. We married in Brinkley. Very few people in this city have lived together longer than we have. July 12, 1938, will make forty-nine years. By July 1939, we will have reached our fiftieth anniversary.

Patrollers, Jayhawkers, Ku Klux, and Ku Klux Klan

"Pateroles, jayhawkers, and the Ku Klux came before the war. The Ku Klux in slavery times were men who would catch Negroes out and keep them if they did not collect from their masters. The pateroles would catch Negroes out and return them if they did not have a pass. They whipped them some- times if they did not have a pass. The jayhawkers were highway men or robbers who stole slaves among other things. At least, that is the way the people regarded them. The jayhawkers stole and pillaged, while the Ku Klux stole those Negroes they caught out. The word 'Klan' was never included in their name.

"The Ku Klux Klan was an organization which arose after the Civil War. It was composed of men who believed in white supremacy and who regulated the morals of the neighborhood. They were not only after Jews and Negroes, but they were sworn to protect the better class of people. They took the law in their own hands.

Slave Work

"I'm not so certain about the amount of work required of slaves. My mother says she picked four hundred pounds of cotton many a day.

The slaves were tasked and given certain amounts to accomplish. I don't know the exact amount nor just how it was determined.

Opinions

"It is too bad that the young Negroes don't know what the old Negroes think and what they have done. The young folks could be helped if they would take advice."

Interviewer's Comment

Badgett's distinctions between jayhawkers, Ku Klux, patrollers, and Ku Klux Klan are most interesting.

I have been slow to catch it. All my life, I have heard persons with ex-slave background refer to the activities of the Ku Klux among slaves prior to 1865. I always thought that they had the Klux Klan and the patrollers confused.

Badgett's definite and clear-cut memories, however, lead me to believe that many of the Negroes who were slaves used the word Ku Klux to denote a type of persons who stole slaves. It was evidently in use before it was applied to the Ku Klux Klan.

The words "Ku Klux" and "Ku Klux Klan" are used indiscriminately in current conversation and literature. It is also true that many persons in the present do, and in the past did, refer to the Ku Klux Klan simply as "Ku Klux."

It is a matter of record that the organization did not at first bear the name "Ku Klux Klan" throughout the South. The name "Ku Klux" seems to have grown in application as the organization changed from a moral association of the best citizens of the South and gradually came under the control of lawless persons with lawless methods--whipping and murdering. It is antecedently reasonable that the change in names accompanying a change in policy would be due to a fitness in the prior use of the name.

The recent use of the name seems mostly imitation and propaganda.

Histories, encyclopedias, and dictionaries, in general, do not record a meaning of the term Ku Klux as prior to the Reconstruction period.

30650

Circumstances of Interview

STATE--Arkansas

NAME OF WORKER--Samuel S. Taylor

ADDRESS--Little Rock, Arkansas

DATE--December, 1938

SUBJECT--Ex-slave

1. Name and address of informant--Jeff Bailey, 713 W. Ninth Street, Little Rock.

2. Date and time of interview--

3. Place of interview--713 W. Ninth Street, Little Rock.

4. Name and address of person, if any, who put you in touch with informant--

5. Name and address of person, if any, accompanying you--

6. Description of room, house, surroundings, etc.

Personal History of Informant

STATE--Arkansas

NAME OF WORKER--Samuel S. Taylor

ADDRESS--Little Rock, Arkansas

DATE--December, 1938

SUBJECT--Ex-slave

NAME AND ADDRESS OF INFORMANT--Jeff Bailey, 713 W. Ninth Street, Little Rock.

1. Ancestry--father, Jeff Wells; mother, Tilda Bailey.

2. Place and date of birth--born in 1861 in Monticello, Arkansas.

3. Family--

4. Places lived in, with dates--reared in Monticello. Lived in Pine Bluff
    thirty-two years, then moved to Little Rock and has lived here thirty-two
    years.

5. Education, with dates--

6. Occupations and accomplishments, with dates--Hostler

7. Special skills and interests--

8. Community and religious activities--

9. Description of informant--

10. Other points gained in interview--

<u>Text of Interview</u> (<u>Unedited</u>)

STATE--Arkansas

NAME OF WORKER--Samuel S. Taylor

ADDRESS--Little Rock, Arkansas

DATE--December, 1938

[A Hostler's Story]

SUBJECT--Ex-slave

NAME AND ADDRESS OF INFORMANT--Jeff Bailey, 713 W. Ninth Street, Little Rock.

* *

"I was born in Monticello. I was raised there. Then I came up to Pine Bluff and stayed there thirty-two years. Then I came up here and been here thirty-two years. That is the reason the white folks so good to me now. I been here so long. I been a hostler all my life. I am the best hostler in this State. I go down to the post office they give me money. These white folks here is good to me.

"What you writin' down? Yes, that's what I said. These white folks like me and they good to me. They give me anything I want. You want a drink? That's the best bonded whiskey money can buy. They gives it to me. Well, if you don't want it now, come in when you do.

"I lost my wife right there in that corner. I was married just once. Lived with her forty-three years. She died here five months ago. Josie Bailey! The white folks thought the world and all of her. That is another reason they give me so much. She was one of the best women I ever seen.

"I gits ten dollars a month. The check comes right up to the house. I used to work with all them money men. Used to handle all them horses at the post office. They ought to give me sixty-five dollars but they don't. But I gits along. God is likely to lemme live ten years longer. I worked

at the post office twenty-two years and don't git but ten dollars a month.
They ought to gimme more.

"My father's name was Jeff Wells. My mother's name was Tilda Bailey.
She was married twice. I took her master's name. Jeff Wells was my father's
name. Governor Bailey ought to give me somethin'. I got the same name he
has. I know him.

"My father's master was Stanley--Jeff Stanley. That was in slavery time.
That was my slave time people. I was just a little bit of a boy. I am
glad you are gittin' that to help the colored people out. Are they goin' to
give the old slaves a pension? What they want to ask all these questions
for then? Well, I guess there's somethin' else besides money that's worth
while.

"My father's master was a good man. He was good to him. Yes Baby!
Jeff Wells, that my father's name. I was a little baby settin' in the
basket 'round in the yard and they would put the cotton all 'round me.
They carried me out where they worked and put me in the basket. I couldn't
pick no cotton because I was too young. When they got through they would
put me in that big old wagon and carry me home. There wasn't no trucks then.
Jeff Wells (that was my father), when they got through pickin' the cotton,
he would say, 'Put them children in the wagon; pick 'em up and put 'em in
the wagon.' I was a little bitty old boy. I couldn't pick no cotton then.
But I used to pick it after the surrender.

"I remember what they said when they freed my father. They said, 'You're
free. You children are free. Go on back there and work and let your chil-
dren work. Don't work them children too long. You'll git pay for your work.'
That was in the Monticello courthouse yard. They said, 'You're free! Free!'

"My mistress said to me when I got back home, 'You're free. Go on out in the orchard and git yoself some peaches.' They had a yard full of peaches. Baby did I git me some peaches. I pulled a bushel of 'em.

Ku Klux Klan

"The Ku Klux run my father out of the fields once. And the white people went and got them 'bout it. They said, 'Times is hard, and we can't have these people losin' time out of the fields. You let these people work.' A week after that, they didn't do no mo. The Ku Klux didn't. Somebody laid them out. I used to go out to the fields and they would ask me, 'Jeff Bailey, what you doin' out here?' I was a little boy and you jus' ought to seen me gittin' 'way frum there. Whooo—eeee!

"I used to pick cotton back yonder in Monticello. I can't pick no cotton now. Naw Lawd! I'm too old. I can't do that kind of work now. I need help. Carl Bailey knows me. He'll help me. I'm a hostler. I handle horses. I used to pick cotton forty years ago. My mother washed clothes right after the War to git us children somethin' to eat. Sometimes somebody would give us somethin' to help us out.

"Tilda Bailey, that was my mother. She and my father belonged to different masters. Bailey was her master's name. She always called herself Bailey and I call myself Bailey. If I die, I'll be Bailey. My insurance is in the name of Bailey. My father and mother had about eight children. They raised all their children in Monticello. You ever been to Monticello? I had a good time in Monticello. I was a baby when peace was declared. Just toddling 'round.

"My father drank too much. I used to tell him about it. I used to
say to him, 'I wouldn't drink so much whiskey.' But he drank it right on.
He drank hisself to death.

"I believe Roosevelt's goin' to be President again. I believe he's
goin' to run for a third term. He's goin' to be dictator. He's goin' to
be king. He's goin' to be a good dictator. We don't want no more Repub-
lic. The people are too hard on the poor people. President Roosevelt lets
everybody git somethin'. I hope he'll git it. I hope he'll be dictator.
I hope he'll be king. Yuh git hold uh some money with him.

"You couldn't ever have a chance if Cook got to be governor. I believe
Carl Bailey's goin' to be a good governor. I believe he'll do better. They
put Miz Carraway back; I believe she'll do good too."

Extra Comment

STATE -- Arkansas

NAME OF WORKER -- Samuel S. Taylor

ADDRESS -- Little Rock, Arkansas

DATE -- December, 1938

SUBJECT -- Ex-slave

NAME AND ADDRESS OF INFORMANT--Jeff Bailey, 713 W. Ninth Street, Little Rock.

* ** ** * * * * * * * * *

Jeff Bailey talked like a man of ninety instead of a man of seventy-six or seven. It was hard to get him to stick to any kind of a story. He had two or three things on his mind and he repeated those things over and over again--Governor Bailey, Hostler, Post Office. He had to be pried loose from them. And he always returned the next sentence.

Interviewer ___Mary D. Hudgins.___

Person Interviewed ___James Baker___ Aged __81__

Home ___With daughter who owns home at 941 Wade St.___

The outskirts of eastern Hot Springs resemble a vast
checkerboard----patterned in Black and White. Within two
blocks of a house made of log-faced siding---painted a
spotless white and provided with blue shutters will be
a shack which appears to have been made from the discard
of a dozen generations of houses.

Some of the yards are thick with rusting cans, old tires
and miscelaneous rubbish. Some of them are so gutted by
gully wash that any attempt at beautification would be worse
than useless. Some are swept---farm fashion---free from
surface dust and twigs. Some attempt---others achieve
grass and flowers. Vegetable gardens are far less frequent
than they should be, considering space left bare.

The interviewer fra kly lost her way several times.
One improper direction took her fully half a mile beyond
her destination. From a hilltop she could look down on
less elevated hills and into narrow valleys. The impression
was that of a cheaply painted back-drop designed for a
"stock" presentation of "Mrs. Wiggs of the Cabbage Patch."

Moving along streets, alleys and paths backward
"toward town" the interviewer reached another hill. Almost
a quarter of a mile away she spied an old colored man
sunning himself on the front porch of a well kept cottage.
Somthing about his white hair and erectly-slumped bearing
screamed "Ex-slave" even at that distance. A negro youth
was passing.

"I beg your pardon, can you tell me where to find
Wade Street and James Baker ?" "Ya--ya--ya---s ma'am.
Dat---dat----dat's de house over da----da---da----da--
r. He---he--he lives at his daughter's" "Could that be
he on the porch ?" Ya---ya----yas ma'am. Dat-----
dat------dat's right."

"Yes, ma'am I'm James Baker. Yes ma'am I remembers
about the war. You want to talk to me about it. Let me
get you a chair. You'd rather sit right there on the step ?
All right ma'am.

I was born in Hot Spring county, below Malvern it
was. I was borned on the farm of a man named Hammonds. But
I was pretty little when he sold me to some folks named Fenton.
Wasn't with them so very long. You know how it goes---back
in them days. When a girl or a boy would marry , why they'd

givem them as many black folks as they could spare. I was give
to one of the daughters when she married. She was Mrs. Samuel
Gentry.

I wasn't so very big before the war. So I didn't have to
work in the fields. Just sort of played around. Can't
remember very much about what happened then. We never did see
no fighting about. They was men what passed through. They
was soldiers. They come backwards and forewards. I was about
as big as th t boy you see there"-----pointing to a lad about
8 years old.-----"some of them they was dressed in blue---sort
of blue. We was told th t they was Federals. Then some of
them was in grey----them was the Southerners.

No, we wasn't scared of them---either of them. They didn't
never bother none of us. Didn't have anything to be sca.ed of
not at all. It wasn't really Malvern we was at----that was
sort of before Malvern come to be. Malvern didn't grow up
until after the railroad come through. The town was across the
river, sort of this side.   It was called Rockport. Ma'am---
you know about Rockport"----a delighted chuckle. "Yes, ma'am.
don't many folks now-a-days know about Rockport. Yes ma'am
the river is pretty shoaly right there. Pretty shoaly.
Yes ma 'am there   was lots of doings around Rockport. Yes
ma'am. Dat's right. Before Garland county was made, Rockport
was the capitol O-----I mean de county seat of Hot Spring

County. Hot Springs was in that county at that time. There
was big doings in town when they held court. Real big doings.

No, ma'am I didn't do nothing much when the war was
over. No, I didn't go to be with my daddy. I moved over to
live with a man I called Uncle Billy----Uncle Billy Bryant
he was. He had all his family with him. I stayed with him
and did what he told me to----'til I grew up. He was always
good to me---treated me like his own children.

Uncle Billy lived at Rockport. I liked living with him.
I remember the court house burned down----or blowed down----
seems like to me it burned down. Uncle Billy got the job of
cleaning bricks. I helped him. That was when they moved
over to Malvern-----the court house I mean. No----no they
didn't. Not then, that was later----they didn't build the
railroad until later. They built it back---sort of simple
like----built it down by Judge Kieth's.

No ma'am. I don't remember nothing about when they
built the railroad. You see we lived across the river---
and I guess----well I just didn't know nothing about it.
But Rockport wasn't no good after the railroad come in.
They moved the court house and most of the folks moved away.
Theyre wasn't nothing much left.

I started farming around there some. I moved about
quite a bit. I lived down sort of by Benton too for quite
a spell. I worked around at most any kind of farming.

'Course most of the time we was working at cotton
and corn. I's spent most of my life farming. I like
it. Moved around pretty considerable. Sometimes I
hired out-----sometimes I share cropped--sometimes
I worked thirds and fourths. What does I mean by
hired out----I means worked for wages. Which way
did I like best----I'll take share-cropping. I sort
of like share-cropping.

I been in Hot Springs for 7 years. Come to be
with my daughter." (An interruption by a small negro
girl---neatly dressed and bright-eyed. Not content
with watching from the sidelines she had edged closer
and squatted comfortably within a couple of feet of
the interviewer. A wide, pearly grin, a wee pointing
forefinger and, "Granddaddy, that lady's got a tablet
just like Aunt Ellen. See, Granddaddy.") "You mustm't
bother the lady. Didn't your mother tell you not to
stop folks when they is talking." ---the voice was
kindly and there was paternal pride in it. A nickle---
tendered the youngster by the interviewer---and
guaranteed to produce a similar tablet won a smile and
childish silence.

Yes, ma'am, I lives with my daughter---her name is
Lulu Mitchell. She owns her house----yes ma'am it helps.
But it's sure hard to get along. Seems like it's lots
harder now than it used to be when I was gitting started.
Lulu works----she irons. Another daughter lives right over
there. Her name's Ellen. She works too---at what she can
get to do. She owns her house too.

Three of my daughters is living. Been married twice--
I has. Didn't stay with the last one long. Yes ma'am I been
coming backwards and forewards to Hot Springs all my life--
you might say. 'Twasn't far over and I kept a'coming back.
Been living all around here. It's pretty nice being with my
daughter. She's good to me. I loves my granddaughter. We has
a pretty hard time----harder dan what I had when I was young---
but then it do seem like it's harder to earn money dan what
it was when I was young. "

Interviewer_____R.S. Taylor_____ _____

Person Interviewed____Uncle William Baltimore_____

Resident__Route #1, Pine Bluff, Arkansas, Jefferson County. Age 103.

"You wants to know how old I is? I'se lived a long time. I'se
goin' on 104. My gran'mammy was over 100 years. My mamma was 100. My
pappy was 96. They was twelve chilluns. I don't know if any of my sisters
or brothers is livin'. Don't know if one of my friends back in my boy
days is livin'. I'se like a poor old leaf left hangin' to a tree.

"Yes - I sho do member back befo' the war. I was borned on the
Dr. Waters place about twleve miles out of Pine Bluff on the east side
of Noble Lake. My gran'mammy and gran'pappy and my mamma and my pappy
were slaves on de Walker plantation. I was not bought or sold- just lived
on de old plantation. I wasn't whipped neither but once I mighty near
got a beatin'. Want to hear about it? I likes to tell.

"Dr. Waters had a good heart. He didn't call us 'slaves'. He call
us 'servants'. He didn't want none of his niggers whipped 'ceptin when
there wasn't no other way. I was grown up pretty good size. Dr. Waters liked
me cause I could make wagons and show mules. Once when he was going away
to be gone all day, he tole me what to do while he was gone. The overseer
wasn't no such good man as old master. He wanted to be boss and told me
what to do. I tole him de big boss had tole me what to do and I was goin'
to do it. He got mad and said if I didn't do what he said I'd take a beating.
I was a big nigger and powerful stout. I tole the overseer fore he whipped me
he's show himself a better man than I was. When he found he was to have a fight
he didn't say no more about the whipping.

"I worked on de plantation till de war broke. Then I went into the army with them what called themselves secesh's. I didn't fight none, never give me a gun nor sword. I was a servant. I cooked and toted things. In 1863 I was captured by the Yankees and marched to Little Rock and sworn in as a Union Soldier. I was sure enough soldier now. I never did any fighting but I marched with the soldiers and worked for them whatever they said.

"We marched from Pine Bluff on through Ft. Smith and the Indian Territory of Oklahoma. Then we went to Leavenworth Kansas and back to Jefferson County, Arkansas. And all that walking I did on these same foots you see right here now.

"On this long march we camped thirty miles from Ft. Smith. We had gone without food three days and was powerful hongry. I started out to get something to eat. I found a sheep, I was tickled. I laughed. I could turn the tast of that sheep meat under my tongue. When I got to camp with the sheep I had to leave for picket duty. Hungrier than ever, I thought of that sheep all the time. When I got back I wanted my chunk of meat. It had been killed, cooked, eat up. Never got a grease spot on my finger from my sheep.

"When time come for breaking up the army I went back to Jefferson county and set to farmin'. I was free now. I didn't do so well on the land as I didn't have mules and money to live on. I went to Dersa County and opened up a blacksmith shop. I learned how to do this work when I was with Dr. Waters. He had me taught by a skilled man. I learned to build wagons too.

"I made my own tools. Who showed me how ? Nobody. When I needed a hack saw I madeit out of a file- that was all I had to make it of. I had to have it. Once I made a cotton scraper out of a piece of hardwood.

I put a steel edge on it. O yes I made everything. "Can I build a wagon-
make all the parts? Every thing but the hubs for the wheels.

"You say I don't seem to see very well. Ha-ha! I don't see nuthin'
at all. I'se been plum blind for 23 years. I can't see nothin'. But I
patches my own clothes. You don't know how I can thread the needle?
Look here. I asked him to let me see his needle threader. He felt around
in a drawer and pulled out a tiny little half arrow which he had made of
a bit of tin with a pair of scissors and fine file. He pushed this through
the eye of the needle, then hooked the thread on it and pulled it back
again threading his needle as fast as if he had good eyesight. This is
a needle threader. I made it myself. Watch me thread a needle. Can't I
do it as fast as if I had a head full of keen eyes? My wife been gone
twenty years. She went blind too. I had to do something. My patches may
not look so pretty but they sure holt (hold).

"You wants to know what I think of the way young folks is doing
these days? They'se goin' to fast. So is their papas and mammas. Dey done
forgot dey's a God and a day of settlin'. Den what dances pays de fid-
dler. I got religion long time ago- jined de Baptist church in 1870 and
haven't never got away from it. I'se tried to tote fair with God and he's
done fair by me.

"Does I get a pension? I shure do. It was a lucky day when de Yankees
got me. Ef they hadn't I don't know what'd become of me. After I went
blind I had hard times. Folks, white folks and all, brought me food. But
that wasn't any good way to get along. Sometimes I ate, sometimes I didn't.
So some of my white, friends dug up my record with the Yankees and got
me a pension. Now I'm setting pretty for de rest of my life.

Yes - O yes I'se older dan most folks get. Still I may be still takin'
my grub here when some of these young whiskey drinkin razzin' around
young chaps is under the dirt. It pays to I don know of any bad spots
in me yet. It pays to live honest, work hard, stay sober. God only
knows what some of these lazy, triflin' drinkin' young folks is comin'
to.

30017

Interviewer_____Pernella M. Anderson_____

Person interviewed_____Mose Banks_____
                    Douglas Addition, El Dorado, Arkansas

Age___69___

- -

"My name is Mose Banks and I am sixty-nine years old. I was born in 1869. I was born four years after freedom but still I was a slave in a way. My papa stayed with his old miss and master after freedom until he died and he just died in 1918, so we all stayed with him too. I had one of the best easiest times in my life. My master was name Bob Stevenson and he was a jewel. Never meaned us, never dogged, never hit one of us in his life. He bought us just like he bought my papa. He never made any of the girls work in the field. He said the work was too hard. He always said splitting rails, bushing, plowing and work like that was for men. That work makes no count women.

"The girls swept yards, cleaned the house, nursed, and washed and ironed, combed old miss' and the children's hair and cut their finger and toe nails and mended the clothes. The womens' job was to cook, attend to the cows, knit all the socks for the men and boys, spin thread, card bats, weave cloth, quilt, sew, scrub and things like that.

"The little boys drove up the cows, slopped the hogs, got wood and pine for light, go to the spring and get water. After a boy was twelve then he let him work in the field. My main job was hitching the horse to the buggy for old Miss Stevenson, and put the saddle on old master's saddle horse.

"I was very small but when the first railroad come through old master took us to see the train. I guess it was about forty or fifty miles

because it took us around four days to make the round trip. The trains
were not like they are now. The engine was smaller and they burned wood
and they had what they called a drum head and they didn't run very fast,
and could not carry many cars. It was a narrow gauge road and the rails
were small and the road was dirt. It was not gravel and rocks like it is
now. It was a great show to me and we all had something to talk about for
a long time. People all around went to see it and we camped out one night
going and coming and camped one night at the railroad so we could see the
train the next day. A man kept putting wood in the furnace in order to
keep a fire. Smoke come out of the drum head. The drum head was something
like a big washpot or a big old hogshead barrel. An ox team was used for
most all traveling. You did not see very many horses or mules.

"The white children taught us how to read and I went to school too.

"I went to church too. We did not have a church house; we used a
brush arbor for service for a long time. In the winter we built a big fire
in the middle and we sat all around the fire on small pine logs. Later
they built a log church, so we had service in there for years.

"We did not live near a school, so old mistress and the children
taught us how to read and write and count. I never went to school in my
life and I bet you, can't none of these children that rub their heads on
college walls beat me reading and counting. You call one and ask them to
divide ninety-nine cows and one bob-tailed bull by two, and they can't
answer it to save their lives without a pencil and paper and two hours'
figuring when it's nothing to say but fifty.

"Wasn't no cook stoves and heaters until about 1890 or 1900. If there
was I did not know about them. They cooked on fireplace and fire out in the yard

on what they called oven and we had plenty of plain grub. We stole eggs
from the big house because we never got any eggs.

"The custom of marrying was just pack up and go on and live with who
you wanted to; that is the Negroes did—I don't know how the white people
married. This lawful marrying came from the law since man made law.

"When anybody died everybody stopped working and moaned and prayed
until after the burying.

"I can say there is as much difference between now and sixty years ago
as it is in day and night."

30608

Interviewer   S. S. Taylor

Person interviewed   Henry Banner
                       County Hospital
Age   ?   Little Rock, Ark.

[Forty Acres and a Mule]

"I was sold the third year of the war for fifteen years old. That would be in 1864. That would make my birthday come in 1849. I must have been 12 year old when the war started and sixteen when Lee surrendered. I was born and raised in Russell County, Ol' Virginny. I was sold out of Russell County during the war. Ol' Man Menefee refugeed me into Tennessee near Knoxville. They sold me down there to a man named Jim Maddison. He carried me down in Virginny near Lynchburg and sold me to Jim Alec Wright. He was the man I was with in the time of the surrender. Then I was in a town called Liberty. The last time I was sold, I sold for $2,300, -- more than I'm worth now.

"Police were for white folks. Patteroles were for niggers. If they caught niggers out without a pass they would whip them. The patteroles were for darkies, police for other people.

"They run me once, and I ran home. I had a dog at home, and there wasn't no chance them gettin' by that dog. They caught me once in Liberty, and Mrs. Charlie Crenchaw, Ol' John Crenchaw's daughter, came out and made them turn me loose. She said, 'They are our darkies; turn them loose.'

"One of them got after me one night. I ran through a gate and he couldn't get through. Every time I looked around,

I would see through the trees some bush or other and think it
was him gaining on me. God knows! I ran myself to death and
got home and fell down on the floor.

"The slaves weren't expecting nothing. It got out some-
how that they were going to give us forty acres and a mule. We
all went up in town. They asked me who I belonged to and I told
them my master was named Banner. One man said, 'Young man, I
would go by my mama's name if I were you.' I told him my mother's
name was Banner too. Then he opened a book and told me all the
laws. He told me never to go by any name except Banner. That
was all the mule they ever give me. ✓

"I started home a year after I got free and made a crop.
I had my gear what I had saved on the plantation and went to
town to get my mule but there wasn't any mule.

"Before the war you belonged to somebody. After the war
you weren't nothin' but a nigger. The laws of the country were
made for the white man. The laws of the North were made for man.

"Freedom is better than slavery though. I done seed both
sides. I seen darkies chained. If a good nigger killed a white
overseer, they wouldn't do nothin' to him. If he was a bad nig-
ger, they'd sell him. They raised niggers to sell; they didn't
want to lose them. It was just like a mule killing a man.

"Yellow niggers didn't sell so well. There weren't so
many of them as there are now. Black niggers stood the climate
better. At least, everybody thought so.

"If a woman didn't breed well, she was put in a gang and
sold. They married just like they do now but they didn't have

no license. Some people say that they done this and that thing
but it's no such a thing. They married just like they do now,
only they didn't have no license.

"Ol' man came out on April 9, 1865, and said, 'General
Lee's whipped now and dam badly whipped. The war is over. The
Yankees done got the country. It is all over. Just go home
and hide everything you got. General Lee's army is coming this
way and stealing everything they can get their hands on.' But
General Lee's army went the other way.

"I saw a sack of money setting near the store. I looked
around and I didn't see nobody. So I took it and carried it
home. Then I hid it. I heard in town that Jeff Davis was dead
and his money was no good. I took out some of the money and
went to the grocery and bought some bread and handed her five
dollar bill. She said, 'My goodness, Henry, that money is no
good; the Yankees have killed it.' And I had done gone all over
the woods and hid that money out. There wasn't no money. No-
body had anything. I worked for two bits a day. All our money
was dead.

"The Yankees fed the white people with hard tacks (at Lib-
erty, Virginia). All around the country, them that didn't have
nothin' had to go to the commissary and get hard tacks.

"I started home. I went to town and rambled all around but
there wasn't nothin' for me.

"I was set free in April. About nine o'clock in the morn-
ing when we went to see what work we would do, ol' man Wright
called us all up and told us to come together. Then he told us
we were free. I couldn't get nothin' to do; so I jus' stayed on
and made a crop."

Interviewer_____Miss Irene Robertson

Person interviewed____John W. H. Barnett, Marianna, Arkansas

Age__81__

- -

"I was born at Clinton Parish, Louisiana. I'm eighty-one years old.
My parents and four children was sold and left six children behind. They
kept the oldest children. In that way I was sold but never alone. Our
family was divided and that brought grief to my parents. We was sold on a
block at New Orleans. J. J. Gambol (Gamble?) in north Louisiana bought us.
After freedom I seen all but one of our family. I don't recollect why that
was.

"For three weeks steady after the surrender people was passing from the
War and for two years off and on somebody come along going home. Some rode
and some had a cane or stick walking. Mother was cooking a pot of shoulder
meat. Them blue soldiers come by and et it up. I didn't get any I know
that. They cleaned us out. Father was born at Eastern Shore, Maryland. He
was about half Indian. Mother's mother was a squaw. I'm more Indian than
Ne/gro. Father said it was a white man's war. He didn't go to war. Mother
was very dark. He spoke a broken tongue.

"We worked on after freedom for the man we was owned by. We worked
crops and patches. I didn't see much difference then. I see a big change
come out of it. We had to work. The work didn't slacken a bit. I never
owned land but my father owned eighty acres in Drew County. I don't know
what become of it. I worked on the railroad section, laid crossties, worked
in stave mills. I farmed a whole lot all along. I hauled and cut wood.

"I get ten dollars and I sells sassafras and little things along to help out. My wife died. My two sons left just before the World War. I never hear from them. I married since then.

"Present times--I can't figure it out. Seems like a stampede. Not much work to do. If I was young I reckon I could find something to do.

"Present generation--Seem like they are more united. The old ones have to teach the young ones what to do. They don't listen all the time. The times is strange. People's children don't do them much good now seems like. They waste most all they make some way. They don't make it regular like we did farming. The work wasn't regular farming but Saturday was ration day and we got that."

Interviewer_____Miss Irene Robertson_____

Person interviewed_____Josephine Ann Barnett_____
                              R.F.D., De Valls Bluff, Arkansas
Age___75 or 80_____

- -

"I do not know$ my exact age. I judge I somewhere between 75 and
80 years old. I was born close to Germantown, Tennessee. We belong,
that is my mother, to Phillip McNeill and Sally McNeill. My mother was
a milker. He had a whole heep of hogs, cattle and stock. That not all
my mother done. She plowed. Childern done the churnin'.

"The way it all come bout I was the onliest chile my mother had.
Him and Miss Sallie left her to help gather the crop and they brought
me in the buggy wid them. I set on a little box in the foot of the
buggy. It had a white umbrella stretched over it. Great big umbrella
run in between them. It was fastened to the buggy seat. When we got to
Memphis they loaded the buggy on the ship. I had a fine time coming.
When we got to Bucks Landing we rode to his place in the buggy. It is
13 miles from here [De Valls Bluff]. In the fall nearly all his slaves
come out here. Then when my mother come on. I never seen my papa after
I left back home ~~(near Germantown)~~. My father belong to Boston Hack.
He wouldn't sell and Mr. McNeill wouldn't sell and that how it come.

"I muster been five or six years old when I come out here to
Arkansas. My grandma was a midwife. She was already out here.
She had to come with the first crowd cause some women was expect-
ing. I tell you it sho was squally times. This country was wild.

It was different from Tennessee or close to Germantown where we come from. None of the slaves liked it but they was brought.

"The war come on direckly after we got here. Several families had the slaves drove off to Texas to save them. Keep em from following the Yankee soldiers right here at the Bluff off. I remember seein' them come up to the gate. My mother and two aunts went. His son and some more men drove em. After freedom them what left childern come back. I stayed with my grandma while they gone. I fed the chickens, shelled corn, churned, swept. I done any little turns they sent me to do.

"One thing I remember happened when they had a scrimmage close — it mighter been the one on Long Prairie — they brought a young boy shot through his lung to Mr. Phillip McNeill's house. He was a stranger. He died. I felt so sorry for him. He was right young. He belong to the Southern army. The Southern army nearly made his place their headquarters.

"Another thing I remember was a agent was going through the country settin' fire to all the cotton. Mr. McNeill had his cotton — all our crop we made. That man set it afire. It burned more than a week big. He burned some left at the gin not Mr. McNeill's. It was fun to us children but I know my grandma cried and all the balance of the slaves. Cause they got some Christmas money and clothes too when the cotton was sold.

"The slaves hated the Yankees. They treated them mean. They was having a big time. They didn't like the slaves. They steal from the slaves too. Some poor folks didn't have slaves.

"After freedom my mother come back after me and we come here to De Valls Bluff and I been here ever since. The Yankee soldiers had built shacks and they left them. They would do. Some was one room, log, boxed and all sorts. They give us a little to eat to keep us from starvin'. It sho was a little bit too. My mother got work about.

"The first schoolhouse was a colored school. We had two rooms and two teachers sent down from the North to teach us. If they had a white school I didn't know it. They had one later on. I was bout grown. Mr. Proctor and Miss Rice was the first teachers. We laughed bout em. They was rough looking, didn't look like white folks down here we'd been used to. They thought they sho was smart. Another teacher come down here was Mr. Abner. White folks wouldn't have nothin' to do with em. We learned. They learned us the ABC's and to write. I can read. I learned a heap of it since I got grown just trying. They gimme a start.

"Times is hard in a way. Prices so high. I never had a hard time in my life. I get $40 a month. It is cause my husband was a soldier here at De Valls Bluff.

"I do not vote. I ain't goiner vote.

"I don't know what to think of the young generation. They are on the road to ruin seems like. I speakin' of the real young folks. They do like they see the white girls and boys doin'. I don't know what to become of em. The women outer stay at home and let the men take care of em. The women seems like taking all the jobs. The colored folks cookin' and making the living for their men folks. It ain't right -- to me. But I don't care how they do. Things ain't got fixed since that last war." [World War].

Interviewer_____Mrs. Rosa B. Ingram_____

Person interviewed___Lizzie Barnett; Conway, Arkansas____

Age___100?___

- -

"Yes, I was born a slave. My old mammy was a slave before me.
She was owned by my old Miss, Fanny Pennington, of Nashville, Ten-
nessee. I was born on a plantation near there. She is dead now. I
shore did love Miss Fanny. "Did you have any brothers and sisters,
Aunt Liz.?" "Why, law yes, honey, my mammy and Miss Fanny raised dey
chillun together. Three each, and we was jes' like brothers and
sisters, all played in de same yard. No, we did not eat together.
Dey sot us niggers out in de yard to eat, but many a night I'se slept
with Miss Fanny.

"Mr. Pennington up and took de old-time consumption. Dey calls it
T. B. now. My mammy nursed him and took it from him and died before
Mr. Abe Lincoln ever sot her free.

"I have seen hard times, Miss, I shore have.

"In dem days when a man owned a plantation and had children and
they liked any of the little slave niggers, they were issued out to
'em just like a horse or cow.

"'Member, honey, when de old-time war happened between the
North and South, The Slavery War. It was so long ago I just can
'member it. Dey had us niggers scared to death of the Bluejackets.
One day a man came to Miss Fanny's house and took a liking to me.

He put me up on a block an' he say, 'How old is dis nigger?' An' she say 'five' when she know well an' good I was ten. No, he didn't get me. But I thought my time had come.

Yes, siree, I was Miss Fanny's child. Why wouldn't I love her when I sucked titty from her breast when my mammy was working in the field? I shore did love Miss Fanny.

When de nigger war was over and dey didn't fit [fight] any longer, Abe Lincoln sot all de niggers free and den got 'sassinated fer doin it.

Miss, you don't know what a hard life we slaves had, cause you ain't old enough to 'member it. Many a time I've heard the bull whips a-flying, and heard the awful cries of the slaves. The flesh would be cut in great gaps and the maggits [maggets] would get in them and they would squirm in misery.

I want you to know I am not an Arkansas born nigger. I come from Tennessee. Be sure to put that down. I moved to Memphis after Miss Fanny died.

While I lived in Memphis, de Yellow Fever broke out. You have never seed the like. Everything was under quarantine. The folks died in piles and de coffins was piled as high as a house. They buried them in trenches, and later they dug graves and buried them. When they got to looking into the coffins, they discovered some had turned over in dey coffins and some had clawed dey eyes out and some had gnawed holes in dey hands. Dey was buried alive!

Miss, do you believe in ha'nts? Well, if you had been in Memphis den you would. Dey was jes' paradin' de streets at nite and you'd meet dem comin at you round de dark corners and all de houses everywhere was ha'nted. I've seed plenty of 'em wid my own eyes, yes, siree.

"Yes, the times were awful in Memphis endurin the plague. Women dead lying around and babies sucking their breasts. As soon as the frost came and the quarantine was lifted, I came to Conway, 1867. But I am a Tennessee nigger.

When I came to Conway there were few houses to live in. No depot. I bought this piece of land to build my shanty from Mr. Jim Harkrider for $25.00. I worked hard for white folks and saved my money and had this little two-room house built [mud chimney, and small porch and one small window]. It is about to fall down on me, but it will last as long as I live. At first, I lived and cooked under a bush [brush] arbor. Cooked on the coals in an iron skillet. Here it is, Miss.

Part ob de time after de nigger war [Civil] I lived in Hot Springs. President 'Kinley had a big reservation over there and a big hospital for the sick and wounded soldiers. Den de war broke out in Cuba and dere was a spatch board ((dispatch)) what de news come over dat de war was on. Den when dat war was over and 'Kinley was tryin to get us niggers a slave pension dey up and 'sassinated him.

After Mr. Lincoln set de slaves free, dey had Northern teachers down South and they were called spies and all left the country.

I don't know 'zactly how old I am. Dey say I am 100. If Miss Fanny was livin' she could settle it. But I have had a hard life. Yes mam. Here I is living in my shanty, 'pendin' on my good white neighbors to feed me and no income 'cept my Old Age Pension. Thank God for Mr. Roosevelt. I love my Southern white friends. I am glad the North and South done shook hands and made friends. All I has to do now is sit and look forward to de day when I can meet my old mammy and Miss Fanny in the Glory Land. Thank God."

Interviewer _____ Miss Irene Robertson

Person interviewed Spencer Barnett (blind), Holly Grove, Ark.

Age   81

- -

"I was born April 30, 1856. It was wrote in a old Bible. I am 81

years old. I was born 3 miles from Florence, Alabama. The folks owned

us was Nancy and Mars Tom Williams. To my recollection they had John,

William, and Tom, boys; Jane, Ann, Lucy, and Emma, girls. In my family

there was 13 children. My parents name Harry and Harriett Barnett.

"Mars Tom Williams had a tanning yard. He bought hides this way:

When a fellow bring hides he would tan em then give him back half what

he brought. Then he work up the rest in shoes, harness, whoops, saddles

and sell them. The men all worked wid him and he had a farm. He

raised corn, cotton, wheat, and oats.

"That slavery was bad. Mars Tom Williams wasn't cruel. He never

broke the skin. When the horn blowed they better be in place. They

used a twisted cowhide whoop. It was wet and tied, then it mortally

would hurt. One thing you had to be in your place day and night. It

was confinin'.

"Sunday was visiting day.

"One man come to dinner, he hit a horse wid a rock and run way.

He missed his dinner. He come back fo dark and went tole Mars Tom.

He didn't whoop him. I was mighty little when that took place.

"They worked on Saturday like any other day. One man fixed out

the rations. It didn't take long fer to go git em.

"The women plowed like men in plow time. Some women made rails. When it was cold and raining they spun and wove in the house. The men cut wood under a shed or side the barn so it knock off the wind. Mars Tom Williams had 12 grown men and women. I was too little to count but I heard my folks call em over by name and number more times en I got fingers and toes. He would hire em out to work some.

"When freedom come on I was on Hawkin Lankford Simpson place. It was 3 or 5 miles from town. They had a big dinner-picnic close by. It was 4 or 5 day of August. A lot of soldiers come by there and said, 'You niggers air free.' It bout broke up the picnic. The white folks broke off home. Them wanted to go back went, them didn't struck off gone wild. Miss Lucy and Mr. Bob Barnett give all of em stayed some corn and a little money. Then he paid off at the end of the year. Then young master went and rented at Dilly Hunt place. We stayed wid him 3 or 4 years then we went to a place he bought. Tom Barnett come to close to Little Rock. Mars William started and died on the way in Memphis. We come on wid the family. Guess they are all dead now. Wisht I know or could find em. Tom never married. He was a soldier. One of the boys died fo the war started.

"My brother Joe married Luvenia Omsted and Lewis Omsted married my sister Betsy and Mars Tom Williams swapped the women. My ma was a cook for the white folks how I come to know so much bout it all. Boys wore loose shirts till they was nine or ten years old. The shirt come to the calf of the leg. No belt.

"We had plenty common eating. They had a big garden and plenty milk. They cooked wid the eggs mostly. They would kill a beef

and have a week of hog killing. They would kill the beef the hardest
weather that come. The families cooked at night and on Sunday at the
log cabins. They cook at night for all next day. The old men hauled
wood.

"When I was a little boy I could hear men runnin' the slaves wid
hounds in the mountains. The landmen paid paddyrollers to keep track
of slaves. Keep em home day and night.

"We took turns bout going to white church. We go in washin' at the
creek and put on clean clothes. She learned me a prayer. Old mistress
learned me to say it nights I slept up at the house. I still can say it:

            'Now I lay me down to sleep
             I pray the Lord my soul to keep
             If I should die fo I wake
             I pray the Lord my soul to take.'

"The slaves at our places had wheat straw beds. The white folks
had fine goose feather beds. We had no idle days. Had a long time at
dinner to rest and rest and water the teams. Sometimes we fed them. Old
mistress had two peafowls roosted in the Colonial poplar trees. She had
a pigeon house and a turkey house. I recken chicken and goose house, too.
When company come you take em to see the farm, the garden, the new leather
things jes' made and to see the little ducks, calves, and colts. Folks
don't care bout seeing that now.

"The girls went to Florence to school. All I can recollect is
them going off to school and I knowed it was Florence.

"The Yankees burned the big house. It was a fine house. Old
mistress moved in the overseer's house. He was a white man. He moved
somewhere else. The Yankees made raids and took 15 or 20 calves from
her at one time. They set the tater house afire. They took the corn.

Old mistress cried more an one time. The Yankees starved out more black faces than white at their stealing. After that war it was hard for the slaves to have a shelter and enough eatin' that winter. They died in piles bout after that August I tole you bout. Joe Innes was our overseer when the house burned.

"The Ku Klux come to my house twice. They couldn't get filled up wid water. They scared us to death. I heard a lot of things they done.

"I don't vote. I voted once in all my life fo some county officers.

"I been in Arkansas since February 5, 1880. I come to Little Cypress. I worked for Mr. Clark by the month, J. W. Crocton's place, Mr. Kitchen's place. I was brakeman on freight train awhile. I worked on the section. I farmed and worked in the timber. I don't have no children; I never been married. I wanted to work by the month all my life. I sells mats (shuck mats) $1.00 and I bottom chairs 50¢. The Social Welfare gives me $10.00. That is 10¢ a meal. That woman next door boards me -- table board -- for 30¢ a day. I make all I can outer fust one thing and another." (He is blind -- cataracts.)

Interviewer_____Miss Irene Robertson

Person interviewed_____Emma Barr, Madison, Arkansas

Age___65___

- -

"My parents belong to two people. Mama was born in Mississippi I think and papa come from North Carolina. Papa's master was Lark Hickerson. Mama was sold from Dr. Ware to Dr. Pope. She was grown when she was sold. She was the mother of twenty-seven children. She had twins three times.

"During the Civil War she was run from the Yankees and had twins on the road. They died or was born dead and she nearly died. They was buried between twin trees close to Hernando, Mississippi. Her last owner was Dr. Pope, ten miles south of Augusta, Arkansas. I was born there and raised up three miles south of Augusta, Arkansas.

"When mama was sold she left her people in Mississippi but after freedom her sisters, Aunt Mariah and Aunt Mary, come here to mama. Aunt Mariah had no children. Aunt Mary had four boys, two girls. She brought her children. Mama said her husband when Dr. Ware owned her was Maxwell but she married my papa after Dr. Pope bought her.

"Dr. Ware had a fine man he bred his colored house women to. They didn't plough and do heavy work. He was hostler, looked after the stock and got in wood. The women hated him, and the men on the place done as well. They hated him too. My papa was a Hickerson. He was a shoemaker and waited on Dr. Pope. Dr. Pope and Miss Marie was good to my parents and to my auntees when they come out here.

"I am the onliest one of mama's children living. Mama was sold on the block and cried off I heard them say when they lived at Wares in Mississippi. Mama was a house girl, Aunt Mary cooked and my oldest sister put fire on the skillet and oven lids. That was her job.

"Mama was lighter than I am. She had Indian blood in her. One auntee was half white. She was lighter than I am, had straight hair; the other auntee was real dark. She spun and wove and knit socks. Mama said they had plenty to eat at both homes. Dr. Pope was good to her. Mama went to the white folks church to look after the babies. They took the babies and all the little children to church in them days.

"Mama said the preachers told the slaves to be good and bedient. The colored folks would meet up wid one another at preaching same as the white folks. I heard my auntees say when the Yankees come to the house the mistress would run give the house women their money and jewelry and soon as the Yankees leave they would come get it. That was at Wares in Mississippi.

"I heard them talk about slipping off and going to some house on the place and other places too and pray for freedom during the War. They turned an iron pot upside down in the room. When some mens' slaves was caught on another man's place he was allowed to whoop them and send them home and they would git another whooping. Some men wouldn't allow that; they said they would tend to their own slaves. So many men had to leave home to go to war times got slack.

"It was Judge Martin that owned my papa before he was freed. He lived close to Augusta, Arkansas. When he was freed he lived at Dr. Pope's. He was sold in North Carolina. Dr. Pope and Judge Martin told them they was free. Mama stayed on with Dr. Pope and he paid her. He never did whoop her,

Mama told me all this. She died a few years ago. She was old. I never heard much about the Ku Klux. Mama was a good speller. I was a good speller at school and she learned with us. I spelled in Webster's Blue Back Speller.

"We children stayed around home till we married off. I nursed nearly all my life. Me and my husband farmed ten years. He died. I don't have a child. I wish I did have a girl. My cousin married us in the church. His name was Andrew Baccus.

"After my husband died I went to Coffeeville, Kansas and nursed an old invalid white woman three years, till she died. I come back here where I was knowed. I'm keeping this house for some people gone off. Part of the house is rented out and I get $8 and commodities. I been sick with the chills."

Interviewer_____S. S. Taylor_____

Person interviewed___Robert Barr_____
                           3108 West 18th St.

Age___73___   Little Rock, Ark.

Occupation_____Preaching_____

- - - - - - - - - [A Preacher Tells His Story]-

"I am a minister of the Gospel. I have been preaching
for the last thirty years. I am batching here. A man does bet-
ter to live by himself. Young people got the devil in them now
a days. Your own children don't want you around.

"I got one grand-daughter that ain't never stood on the
floor. Her husband kicked her and hit her and she ain't never
been able to stand up since. I got another daughter that ain't
thinking about marrying. She just goes from one man to the
other.

"The government gives me a pension. The white folks help
me all along. Before I preached, I fiddled, danced, shot craps,
did anything.

"My mother was born in Chickasaw, Mississippi. She was
born a slave. Old man Barr was her master. She was a Lucy
Appelin and she married a Barr. I don't know whether she stood
on the floor and married then as they do now or not. They tell
me that they just gave them to them in those days. My mother
said that they didn't know anything about marriage then. They
had some sort of a way of doing. Ol' Massa would call them up
and say, 'You take that man, and go ahead. You are man and wife.'
I don't care whether you liked it or didn't. You had to go

ahead. I heard em say: 'Nigger ain't no more'n a horse or cow.' But they got out from under that now. The world is growing more and more civilized. But when a nigger thinks he is something, he ain't nothin'. White folks got all the laws and regulations in their hands and they can do as they please. You surrender under em and go along and you are all right. If they told a woman to go to a man and she didn't, they would whip her. You didn't have your own way. They would make you do what they wanted. They'd give you a good beating too.

"My father was born in Mississippi. His name was Simon Barr. My mother and father both lived on the same plantation. In all groups of people they went by their master's name. Before she married, my mother's master and mistress were Appelins. When she got married - got ready to marry - the white folks agreed to let them go together. Old Man Barr must have paid something for her. According to my mother and father, that's the way it was. She had to leave her master and go with her husband's master.

"According to my old father and mother, the Patteroles went and got the niggers when they did something wrong. They lived during slave time. They had a rule and government over the colored and there you are. When they caught niggers out, they would beat them. If you'd run away, they'd go and get you and beat you and put you back. When they'd get on a nigger and beat him, the colored folks would holler, 'I pray, Massa.' They had to have a great war over it, before they freed the nigger. The Bible says there is a time for all things.

"My mother and father said they got a certain amount when

they was freed. I don't know how much it was. It was only a small amount. After a short time it broke up and they didn't get any more. I get ten dollars pension now and that is more than they got then.

"I heard Old Brother Page in Mississippi say that the slaves had heard em say they were going to be free. His young mistress heard em say he was going to be free and she walked up and hocked and spit in his face. When freedom came, old Massa came out and told them.

"I have heard folks talk of buried treasure. I'll bet there's more money under the ground than there is on it. They didn't have banks then, and they put their money under the ground. For hundreds of years, there has been money put under the ground.

"I heard my mother talk about their dances and frolics then. I never heard her speak of anything else. They didn't have much freedom. They couldn't go and come as they pleased. You had to have a script to go and come. Niggers ain't free now. You can't do anything; you got nothin'. This whole town belongs to white folks, and you can't do nothin'. If nigger get to have anything, white folks will take it.

"We raised our own food. We made our own flour. We wove our own cloth. We made our clothes. We made our meal. We made our sorghum cane molasses. Some of them made their shoes, made their own medicine, and went around and doctored on one another. They were more healthy then than they are now. This generation don't live hardly to get forty years old. They don't live long now.

"I came to Arkansas about thirty-five years ago. I got right into ditches. The first thing I did was farm. I farmed about ten years. I made about ten crops. Mississippi gave you more for your crops than Arkansas."

Interviewer_____Mrs. Bernice Bowden_____

Person interviewed_____Matilda Bass_____
1100 Palm Street, Pine Bluff, Arkansas

Age__80__

- -

"Yes ma'am, I was eight years old when the Old War ceasted.

"Honey, I've lived here twenty years and I don't know what this street is.

"I was born in Greenville, Mississippi. They took my parents and carried 'em to Texas to keep 'em from the Yankees. I think they stayed three years 'cause I didn't know 'em when they come back.

"I 'member the Yankees come and took us chillun and the old folks to Vicksburg. I 'member the old man that seed after the chillun while their parents was gone, he said I was eight when freedom come. We didn't know nothin' 'bout our ages--didn't have 'nough sense.

"My parents come back after surrender and stayed on my owner's place--John Scott's place. We had three masters--three brothers.

"I been in Arkansas twenty years--right here. I bought this home.

"I married my husband in Mississippi. We farmed.

"The Lord uses me as a prophet and after my husband died, the Lord sent me to Arkansas to tell the people. He called me out of the church. I been out of the church now thirty-three years. Seems like all they think about in the churches now is money, so the Lord called me out."

Interviewer_____Miss Irene Robertson_____

Person interviewed_____Emmett Beal, Biscoe, Arkansas_____

Age___78___

- -

"I was born in Holloman County, Bolivar, Tennessee. Master Dr. Jim May owned my set er folks. He had two girls and two boys. I reckon he had a wife but I don't recollect seeing her. Ma suckled me; William May with me. Ely and Seley and Susie was his children.

"I churned for mama in slavery. She tied a cloth around the top so no flies get in. I better hadn't let no fly get in the churn. She take me out to a peach tree and learn me how to keep the flies outen the churn next time.

"Mama was Dr. May's cook. We et out the dishes but I don't know how all of 'em done their eating. They eat at their houses. Dr. May had a good size bunch of hands, not a big crowd. We had straw beds. Made new ones every summer. In that country they didn't 'low you to beat yo' hands up. I heard my folks say that more'n one time.

"Dr. May come tole 'em it was freedom. They could get land and stay— all 'at wanted to. All his old ones kept on wid him. They sharecropped and some of them got a third. I recollect him and worked for him.

"The Ku Klux didn't bother none of us. Dr. May wouldn't 'low them on his place.

"Mama come out here in 1880. I figured there better land out here and I followed her in 1881. We paid our own ways. Seem like the owners ought to give the slaves something but seem like they was mad 'cause they set us free. Ma was named Viney May and pa, Nick May.

"Pa and four or five brothers was sold in Memphis. He never seen his brothers no more. They come to Arkansas.

"Pa and Dr. May went to war. The Yankees drafted pa and he come back to Dr. May after he fit. He got his lip split open in the War. Dr. May come home and worked his slaves. He didn't stay long in war.

"I reckon they had plenty to eat at home. They didn't run to the stores every day 'bout starved to death like I has to do now. Ma said they didn't 'low the overseers to whoop too much er Dr. May would turn them off.

"Er horse stomped on my foot eight years ago. I didn't pay it much 'tention. It didn't hurt. Blood-p'ison come in it and they took me to the horsepital and my leg had to come off, (at the knee).

"We have to go back to Africa to vote all the 'lections. Voting brings up more hard feelings."

Interviewer
Pernella Anderson, colored.

EX-SLAVES

Yes I was born in slavery time. I was born September 2, 1862 in the field under a tree. I don't know nothing about slavery. I was too young to remember anything about slavery. But I tell you this much, times ain't like they used to be. There was easy living back in the 18 hundred years. People wore homemade clothes, what I mean homespun and lowell clothes. My ma spun and weaved all of her cloth. We wore our dresses down to our ankles in length and my dresses was called mother hubbards. The skirts had about three yards circumference and we wore plenty of clothes under our dress. We did not go necked like these folks do now. Folk did not know how we was made. We did not show our shape, we did not disgrace ourself back in 1800. We wore our hair wrapped and head rags tied on our head. I went barefooted until I was a young missie then I wore shoes in the winter but I still went barefooted in the summer. My papa was a shoemaker so he made our shoes. We raised everything that we ate when I was a chap. We ate a plenty. We raised plenty of whippowell peas. That was the only kind of peas there was then. We raised plenty Moodie sweet potatoes they call them nigger chokers now. We had cows so we had plenty of milk and butter. We cooked on the fireplace. The first stove I cooked on was a white woman's stove, that was 1890.

I never chanced to go to school because where we lived there wasn't no school. I worked all of the time. In fact that was all we knew. White people did not see where negroes needed any learning so we had to work. We lived on a place with some white people by the name of Dunn. They were good people but they taken all that was made because we did not know. I ain't never been sick in my life and I have never had a doctor in my life. I am in good health now.

We traveled horseback in the years of 1800. We did not ride straddle the horse's back we rode sideways. The old folks wore their dreses dragging the ground. We chaps called everybody old that married. We respected them because they was considered

as being old. Time has made a change.

-Dina Beard, Douglas Addition.

Interviewer_____Miss Irene Robertson_____

Person interviewed____Annie Beck, West Memphis, Arkansas

Age___50___

- -

"I was born in Mississippi.
Mama was born in Alabama and sold
to Holcomb, Mississippi. Her owner
was Master Beard. She was a field
woman. They took her in a stage-
coach. Their owner wanted to keep
it a secret about freedom. But he
had a brother that fussed with him
all the time and he told the
slaves they was all free. Mama
said they was pretty good always
to her for it to be slavery, but
papa said his owners wasn't so
good to him. He was sold in Rich-
mond, Virginia to Master Thomas at
Grenada, Mississippi. He was a
plain farming man."

Interviewer _____ Bernice Bowden _____

Person interviewed   J. H. Beckwith _____
                      619 North Spruce Street, Pine Bluff, Arkansas

Age 68

- -

"No ma'm I was not born in the time of slavery. I was sixty-eight last Friday. I was born November 18, 1870 in Johnson County, North Carolina.

"My mother was born in Georgia and her name was Gracie Barum. Father was born in North Carolina. His name was Rufus Beckwith. He belonged to Doctor Beckwith and mother, I think, belonged to Tom Barum. Barum was just an ordinary farmer. He was just a second or third class farmer -- just poor white folks. I think my mother was the only slave he owned.

My father had to walk seven miles every Saturday night to see my mother, and be back before sunrise Monday.

"My parents had at least three or four children born in slavery. I know my father said he worked at night and made shoes for his family.

"My father was a mulatto. He had a negro mother and a white father. He had a mechanical talent. He seemed to be somewhat of a genius. He had a productive mind. He could do blacksmithing, carpenter work, brick work and shoe work.

"Father was married twice. He raised ten children by each wife. I think my mother had fifteen children and I was the the thirteenth child. I am the only boy among the first set, called to the ministry. And there was one in the second set. Father learned to read and write after freedom.

"After freedom he sent my oldest brother and sister to Hampton, Virginia and they were graduated from Hampton Institute and later taught school. They were graduated from the same school Booker T. Washington was. He got his idea of vocational education there.

"I haven't had much education. I went as far as the eighth grade. The biggest education. I have had was in the Conference.

"I joined the Little Rock General Conference at Texarkana in 1914. This was the Methodist Episcopal, North, and I was ordained as a deacon and later an elder by white bishops. Then in 1930 I joined the African Methodist.

"By trade I am a carpenter and bricklayer. I served an apprentice under my father and under a German contractor.

"I used to be called the best negro journeyman carpenter between Monroe, Louisiana and Little Rock, Arkansas.

"I made quite a success in my trade. I have a couple of United States Patent Rights. One is a brick mold holding ten bricks and used to make bricks of concrete. The other is a sliding door. (See attached drawings)

"I was in the mercantile business two and one-half years in Sevier County. I sold that because it was too confining and returned to the carpenter's trade. I still practice my trade some now.

"I have not had to ask help from anyone. I have helped others. I own my home and I sent my daughter to Fisk University where she was graduated. While there she met a young man and they were later married and now live in Chicago. They own their home and are doing well.

"In my work in the ministry I am trying to teach my people to have higher ideals. We have to bring our race to that high ideal of race integrity. I am trying to keep the negro from thinking he is hated by the upper class of white people. What the negro needs is self-consciousness to the extent that he aspires to the higher principles in order to stand on an equal plane in attainment but not in a social way.

"At present, the negro's ideals are too low for him to visualize the evils involved in race mixture. He needs to be lifted in his own estimation and learn that a race cannot be estimated by other races — by anything else but their own ideals.

"The younger generation is off on a tangent. They'll have to hit something before they stop.

"The salvation of our people -- of all people—white and colored, is leadership. We've got to have vision and try to give the people vision. Not to live for ourselves but for all. The present generation is selfish. The life should flow out and as it flows out it makes room for more life. If It does not flow out, it congeals and ferments. Selfishness is just like damming a stream.

"I think Woodrow Wilson won the World War with his fourteen points of democracy. If the people of foreign countries had not that old imperialism sentiment, the Jew would not be where he is today."

Interviewer's Comment

This man is the best informed and most sensible negro I have interviewed. In the room where I interviewed him, were a piano, a radio, many ferns, a wool rug, chairs, divan, and a table on which were books including a set of the Standard History of the World. I asked if he had read the history and he replied, "Not all of it but I have read the volumes pertaining to the neolithic age."

On the walls were several pictures and two tapestries.

The house was a good frame one and electric current was used.

Interviewer_____Miss Irene Robertson

Person interviewed Enoch Beel; Green Grove, Hazen, Arkansas

Age___79___

- -

"Yes maam I was born a slave, born in slavery times. I wer born in Hardman County, Tennessee. My own daddy was a Union soldier and my mama was a cook fer the mistress. We belonged to Miss Viney and Dr. Jim Mass. My daddy drawed a pension fer bein a soldier till he die. He went off to wait on some men he know. Then he met some men wanted him to join the army. They said then he get paid and get a bounty. No maam he never got a red cent. He come back broke as he went off. He say he turned loose soon as he could and mustered out and lef them right now. He had no time to ax em no questions. That what he said! We stayed on that place till I was big nuf to do a days work. We had no other place to go. There was plenty land and no stock. Houses to stay in got scarce. If a famley had a place to stay at when that war ended he counted hisself lucky I tell you. Heap of black an white jes ramlin round through the woods an over the roads huntin a little to eat or a little sumpin to do. If you stay in the field workin about puttin back the fences an round yo own house you wouldn't be hurt.

"The Ku Kluxes war not huntin work theirselves. They was keepin order at the gatherins and down the public roads. Folks had come toted off all the folks made in the crops till they don't call nuthin stealin.

They whooped em and made em ride on rails. I don't know all the car-
rings on did take place. I sho would been scared if I seed em comin to
me. We left Dr. Mass and went to Grain, Tennessee. I had three sisters
and half-brothers. I don't remember how many, some dead. I farmed all
my life. Everybody said the land was so much better and newer out in
Arkansas. When I married I come to Tomberlin and worked fer Sam Dardnne
bout twelve years. Then I rented from Jim Hicks at England. I rented
from one of the Carlley boys and Jim Neelam. When I very fust come here
I worked at Helena on a farm one year. When I got my leg taken off it
cost bout all I ever had cumlated. I lives on my sister's place. Henry
Bratcher's wife out at Green Grove. The Wellfare give me $8 cause I
caint get bout.

"I don't know bout the times. It is so unsettled. Folks want work
caint get it and some won't work that could. You caint get help so you
can make a crop of your own no more, fer sometimes is close."

Interviewer_____Miss Irene Robertson_____

Person interviewed___Sophie D. Belle, Forrest City, Arkansas_____

Age___77___

- -

"I was born near Knoxville, Georgia. My mother was a professional pastry cook. She was a house woman during slavery. She was owned by Lewis Hicks and Ann Hicks. They had Saluda, Mary, Lewis, and Oscar.

"Mother was never sold. Mr. Hicks reared her. She was three-fourths Indian. Her father was George Hicks. Gordon carried him to Texas. Mr. Bob Gordon was mean. He asked Mr. Hicks to keep mother and auntie while he went to Texas. Mr. Gordon was so mean. My mother had two little girls but my sister died while small.

"I never saw any one sold. I never saw a soldier. But I noticed the grown people whispering many times. Mother explained it to me, they had some news from the War. Aunt Jane said she saw them pass in gangs. I heard her say, 'Did you see the soldiers pass early this morning?' I was asleep. Sometimes I was out at play when they passed.

"Master Hicks called us all up at dinner one day to the big house. He told us, 'You are free as I am.' I never had worked any then. No, they cried and went on to their homes. Aunt Jane was bad to speak out, she was so much Indian. She had three children. She went to another place to live. She was in search of her husband and thought he might be there at Ft. Valley.

"Mother stayed on another year. Mr. Hicks was good to us. None of the children ever worked till they was ten or twelve years old.

He had a lot of slaves and about twenty-five children on the place growing.
He had just a big plantation. He had a special cook, Aunt Mariah, to cook
for the field hands. They eat like he did. Master Hicks would examine
their buckets and a great big split basket. If they didn't have enough to
eat he would have her cook more and send to them. They had nice victuals to
eat. He had a bell to ring for all the children to be put to bed at sundown
and they slept late. He said, 'Let them grow.' Their diet was milk and
bread and eggs. We had duck eggs, guinea eggs, goose eggs, and turkey eggs.

"I don't know what all the slaves had but mother had feather beds.
They saved all kind of feathers to make pillows and bed and chair cushions.
We always had a pet pig about our place. Master Hicks kept a drove of pea-
fowls. He had cows, goats, sheep. We children loved the lambs. Elvira
attended to the milk. She had some of the girls and boys to milk. Uncle
Dick, mother's brother, was Mr. Hicks' coachman. He was raised on the
place too.

"I think Master Hicks and his family was French, but, though they were
light-skin people. They had light hair too, I think.

"One day a Frenchman (white) that was a doctor come to call. My Aunt
Jane said to me, 'He is your papa. That is your papa.' I saw him many
times after that. I am considered eight-ninth white race. One little girl
up at the courthouse asked me a question and I told her she was too young to
know about such sin. (This girl was twenty-four years old and the case
worker's stenographer.)

"Master Hicks had Uncle Patrick bury his silver and gold in the woods.
It was in a trunk. The hair and hide was still on the trunk when the War
ceased. He used his money to pay the slaves that worked on his place after
freedom.

"I went to school to a white man from January till May and mother paid him one dollar a month tuition. After I married I went to school three terms. I married quite young. Everyone did that far back.

"I married at Aunt Jane's home. We got married and had dinner at one or two o'clock. Very quiet. Only a few friends and my relatives. I wore a green wool traveling dress. It was trimmed in black velvet and black beads. I married in a hat. At about seven o'clock we went to my husband's home at Perry, Georgia. He owned a new buggy. We rode thirty miles. We had a colored minister to marry us. He was a painter and a fine provider. He died. I had no children.

"I came to Forrest City 1874. There was three dry-goods and grocery stores and two saloons here--five stores in all. I come alone. Aunt Jane and Uncle Sol had migrated here. My mother come with me. There was one railroad through here. I belong to the Baptist church.

"I married the second time at Muskogee, Oklahoma. My husband lived out there. He was Indian-African. He was a Baptist minister. We never had any children. I never had a child. They tell me now if I had married dark men I would maybe had children. I married very light men both times.

"I washed and ironed, cooked and kept house. I sewed for the public, black and white. I washed and ironed for Mrs. Graham at Crockettsville twenty-three years and three months. I inherited a home here. Owned a home here in Forrest City once. I live with my cousin here. He uses that house for his study. He is a Baptist minister. (The church is in front of their home--a very nice new brick church -- ed.) I'm blind now or I could still sew, wash and iron some maybe.

"I get eight dollars from the Social Welfare. I do my own cooking in the kitchen. I am seventy-seven years old. I try to live as good as my age. Every year I try to live a little better, 'A little sweeter as the years go by.' "

Interviewer_____Samuel S. Taylor

Person interviewed_____Cyrus Bellus
                           1320 Pulaski Street, Little Rock, Arkansas
Age 73

[Made Own Cloth]

- -

"I was born in Mississippi in 1865 in Jefferson County. It was on the tenth of March. My father's name was Cyrus Bellus, the same as mine. My mother's name was Matilda Bellus.

"My father's master was David Hunt. My father and mother both belonged to him. They had the same master. I don't know the names of my grandfather and mother. I think they were Jordans. No, I know my grandmother's name was Annie Hall, and my grandfather's name was Stephen Hall. Those were my mother's grandparents. My father's father was named John Major and his mother was named Dinah Major. They belonged to the Hunts. I don't know why the names was different. I guess he wasn't their first master.

Slave Sales, Whippings, Work

"I have heard my folks talk about how they were traded off and how they used to have to work. Their master wouldn't allow them to whip his hands. No, it was the mistress that wouldn't allow them to be whipped. They had hot words about that sometimes.

"The slaves had to weave cotton and knit sox. Sometimes they would work all night, weaving cloth, and spinning thread. The spinning would be done first. They would make cloth for all the hands on the place.

"They used to have tanning vats to make shoes with too. Old master didn't know what it was to buy shoes. Had a man there to make them.

"My father and mother were both field hands. They didn't weave or
spin. My grandmother on my mother's side did that. They were supposed to
pick--the man, four hundred pounds of cotton, and the woman three hundred.
And that was gittin' some cotton. If they didn't come up to the task, they
was took out and give a whipping. The overseer would do the thrashing.
The old mistress and master wouldn't agree on that whipping.

Fun

"The slaves were allowed to get out and have their fun and play and
'musement for so many hours. Outside of those hours, they had to be found
in their house. They had to use fiddles. They had dancing just like the
boys do now. They had knockin' and rasslin' and all such like now.

Church

"So far as serving God was concerned, they had to take a kettle and
turn it down bottom upward and then old master couldn't hear the singing
and prayin'. I don't know just how they turned the kettle to keep the
noise from goin' out. But I heard my father and mother say they did it.
The kettle would be on the inside of the cabin, not on the outside.

House, Furniture, Food

"The slaves lived in log houses instead of ones like now with weather-
boarding. The two ends duffed in. They always had them so they would hold
a nice family. Never had any partitions to make rooms. It was just a
straight long house with one window and one door.

"Provisions were weighed out to them. They were allowed
four pounds of meat and a peck of meal for each working person.

They only provided for the working folks. If I had eight in a family, I would just get the same amount. There was no provisions for children.

"But all the children on the place were given something from the big house. The working folks ate their breakfast before daylight in the log cabin where they lived. They ate their supper at home too. They was allowed to get back home by seven or eight o'clock. The slaves on my place never ate together. I don't know anything about that kind of feeding.

"They had nurses, old folks that weren't able to work any longer. All the children would go to the same place to be cared for and the old people would look after them. They wasn't able to work, you know. They fed the children during the day.

How Freedom Came

"My father and mother and grandmother said the overseer told them that they were free. I guess that was in 1865, the same year I was born. The overseer told them that they didn't have any owner now. They was free folks. The boss man told them too--had them to come up to the big house and told them they had to look out for themselves now because they were free as he was.

Right After the War

"Right after emancipation, my folks were freed. The boss man told them they could work by the day or sharecrop or they could work by groups. A group of folks could go together and work and the boss man would pay them so much a day. I believe they worked for him a good while--about seven or eight years at least. They was in one of the groups.

Earliest Recollections

"My own earliest recollections was of picking cotton in one of those squads--the groups I was telling you about. After that, the people got to renting land and renting stock for themselves. They sharecropped then. It seems to me that everybody was satisfied. I don't remember any one saying that he was cheated or beat out of anything.

Schooling

"We had a public school to open in Jefferson County, Mississippi. We called it Dobbins Bridge. There was a bridge about a mile long built across the creek. We had two colored women for teachers. Their names was Mary Howard and Hester Harris. They only used two teachers in that school. I attended there three years to those same two women.

"We had a large family and I quit to help take care of it.

Ku Klux

"I don't think there was much disturbance from the Ku Klux on that plantation. The colored folks didn't take much part in politics.

Later Life

"I stopped school and went to work for good at about fifteen years. I worked at the field on that same plantation I told you about. I worked there for just about ten years. Then I farmed at the same place on shares. I stayed there till I was 'bout twenty-six years old. Then I moved to Wilderness Place in the Cotton Belt in Mississippi. I farmed there for two years.

"I farmed around Greenville, Mississippi for a while. Then I left Greenville and came to Arkansas. I came straight to Little Rock.

The first thing I did I went into the lumber grading. I wasn't trained to it, but I went into it at the request of the men who employed me. I stayed in that eight years. I learned the lumber grading and checking. Checking is seeing the size and width and length and kind of lumber and seeing how much of it there is in a car without taking it out, you know.

"I married about 1932. My wife is dead. We never had any children.

"I haven't worked any now in five years. I have been to the hospital in the east end. I get old age assistance--eight dollars and commodities."

Interviewer_____Mrs. Bernice Bowden_____

Person interviewed_____Bob Benford_____
209 N. Maple Street, Pine Bluff, Arkansas

Age__79__

- -

"Slavery-time folks? Here's one of em. Near as I can get at it, I'se seventy-nine. I was born in Alabama. My white folks said I come from Perry County, Alabama, but I come here to this Arkansas country when I was small.

"My old master was Jim Ad Benford. He was good to us. I'm goin' to tell you we was better off then than now. Yes ma'am, they treated us right. We didn't have to worry bout payin' the doctor and had plenty to eat.

"I recollect the shoemaker come and measured my feet and directly he'd bring me old red russet shoes. I thought they was the prettiest things I ever saw in my life.

"Old mistress would say, 'Come on here, you little niggers' and she'd sprinkle sugar on the meat block and we'd just lick sugar.

"I remember the soldiers good, had on blue suits with brass buttons.

"I'se big enough to ride old master's hoss to water. He'd say, 'Now, Bob, don't you run that hoss' but when I got out of sight, I was bound to run that hoss a little.

"I didn't have to work, just stayed in the house with my mammy. She was a seamstress. I'm tellin' you the truth now. I can tell it at night as well as daytime.

"We lived in Union County. Old master had a lot of hands. Old mistress' name was Miss Sallie Benford. She just as good as she could be. She'd come out to the quarters to see how we was gettin' along.

I'd be so glad when Christmas come. We'd have hog killin' and I'd get the bladders and blow em up to make noise -- you know. Yes, lady, we'd have a time.

"I recollect when Marse Jim broke up and went to Texas. Stayed there bout a year and come back.

"When the war was over I recollect they said we was free but I didn't know what that meant. I was always free.

"After freedom mammy stayed there on the place and worked on the shares. I don't know nothin' bout my father. They said he was a white man.

"I remember I was out in the field with mammy and had a old mule. I punched him with a stick and he come back with them hoofs and kicked me right in the jaw -- knocked me dead. Lord, lady, I had to eat mush till I don't like mush today. That was old Mose -- he was a saddle mule.

"Me? I ain't been to school a day in my life. If I had a chance to go I didn't know it. I had to help mammy work. I recollect one time when she was sick I got into a fight and she cried and said, 'That's the way you does my child' and I know she died next week.

"After that I worked here and there. I remember the first man I worked for was Kinch McKinney of El Dorado.

"I remember when I was just learnin' to plow, old mule knew five hundred times more than I did. He was graduated and he learnt me.

"I made fifty-seven crops in my lifetime. Me and Hance Chapman -- he was my witness when I married -- we made four bales that year. That was in 1879. His father got two bales and Hance and me got two. I made money every year. Yes ma'am, I have made some money in my day. When I moved from Louisiana to Arkansas I sold one hundred eighty acres of land and three hundred head of hogs. I come up here cause my chillun was here and my wife wanted to come here. You know how people will stroll when they get grown. Lost everything I had. Bought a little farm here and they wouldn't let me raise but two acres of cotton the last year I farmed and I couldn't make my payments with that. Made me plow up some of the prettiest cotton I ever saw and I never got a cent for it.

"Lady, nobody don't know how old people is treated nowdays. But I'm livin' and I thank the Lord. I'm so glad the Lord sent you here, lady. I been once a man and twice a child. You know when you're tellin' the truth, you can tell it all the time.

"Klu Klux? The Lord have mercy! In '74 and '75 saw em but never was bothered by a white man in my life. Never been arrested and never had a lawsuit in my life. I can go down here and talk to these officers any time.

"Yes ma'am, I used to vote. Never had no trouble. I don't know what ticket I voted. We just voted for the man we wanted. Used to have colored men on the grand jury -- half and half -- and then got down to one and then knocked em all out.

"I never done no public work in my life but when you said farmin' you hit me then.

"Nother thing I never done. I bought two counterpins once in my life on the stallments and ain't never bought nothin' since that way. Yes ma'am, I got a bait of that stallment buying. That's been forty years ago.

"I know one time when I was livin' in Louisiana, we had a teacher named Arvin Nichols. He taught there seventeen years and one time he passed some white ladies and tipped his hat and went on and fore sundown they had him arrested. Some of the white men who knew him went to court and said what had he done, and they cleared him right away. That was in the '80's in Marion, Louisiana, in Union Parish."

30757

Interviewer_____Miss Irene Robertson_____

Person interviewed__Carrie Bradley Logan Bennet, Helena, Arkansas

Age__79 plus___

- -

"I was born not a great piece from Mobile but it was in Mississippi in the country. My mother b'long to Massa Tom Logan. He was a horse trader. He got drowned in 1863--durin' of the War, the old war. His wife was Miss Liza Jane. They had several children and some gone from home I jus' seed when they be on visits home. The ones at home I can recollect was Tiney, John, Bill, and Alex. I played wid Tiney and nursed Bill and Alex was a baby when Massa Tom got drowned.

"We never knowed how Massa Tom got drowned. They brought him home and buried him. His horse come home. He had been in the water, water was froze on the saddle. They said it was water soaked. They thought he swum the branch. Massa Tom drunk some. We never did know what did happen. I didn't know much 'bout 'em.

"He had two or three families of slaves. Ma cooked, washed and ironed for all on the place. She went to the field in busy times. Three of the men drove horses, tended to 'em. They fed 'em and curried and sheared 'em. Ma said Massa Tom sure thought a heap of his niggers and fine stock. They'd bring in three or four droves of horses and mules, care fer 'em, take 'em out sell 'em. They go out and get droves, feed 'em up till they looked like different from what you see come there. He'd sell 'em in the early part of the year. He did make money. I know he muster. My pa was the head black-smith on Massa Tom's place, them other men helped him along.

"I heard ma say no better hearted man ever live than Massa Tom if you ketch him sober. He give his men a drink whiskey 'round every once in awhile. I don't know what Miss Liza Jane could do 'bout it. She never done nothin' as ever I knowed. They sent apples off to the press and all of us drunk much cider when it come home as we could hold and had some long as it lasts. It turn to vinegar. I heard my pa laughing 'bout the time Massa Tom had the Blue Devils. He was p'isoned well as I understood it. It muster been on whiskey and something else. I never knowed it. His men had to take keer of 'em. He acted so much like he be crazy they laughed 'bout things he do. He got over it.

"Old mistress—we all called her Miss Liza Jane—whooped us when she wanted to. She brush us all out wid the broom, tell us go build a play house. Children made the prettiest kinds of play houses them days. We made the walls outer bark sometimes. We jus' marked it off on the ground out back of the smokehouse. We'd ride and bring up the cows. We'd take the meal to a mill. It was the best hoecake bread can be made. It was water ground meal.

"We had a plenty to eat, jus' common eatin'. We had good cane molasses all the time. The clothes was thin 'bout all time 'ceptin' when they be new and stubby. We got new clothes in the fall of the year. They last till next year.

"I never seed Massa Tom whoop nobody. I seen Miss Liza Jane turn up the little children's dresses and whoop 'em with a little switch, and straws, and her hand. She 'most blister you wid her bare hand. Plenty things we done to get whoopin's. We leave the gates open; we'd run the calves and try to ride 'em; we'd chunk at the geese. One thing that make her so mad was for us to climb up in her fruit trees and break off a limb.

She wouldn't let us be eating the green fruit mostly 'cause it would make us sick. They had plenty trees. We had plenty fruit to eat when it was ripe. Massa Tom's little colored boys have big ears. He'd pull 'em every time he pass one of 'em. He didn't hurt 'em but it might have made their ears stick out. They all had big ears. He never slapped nobody as ever I heard 'bout.

"I don't know how my parents was sold. I'm sure they was sold. Pa's name was Jim Bradley (Bradly). He come from one of the Carolinas. Ma was brought to Mississippi from Georgia. All the name I heard fer her was Ella Logan. When freedom come on, I heard pa say he thought he stand a chance to find his folks and them to find him if he be called Bradley. He did find some of his brothers, and ma had some of her folks out in Mississippi. They come out here hunting places to do better. They wasn't no Bradleys. I was little and I don't recollect their names. Seem lack one family we called Aunt Mandy Thornton. One was Aunt Tillie and Uncle Mack. They wasn't Thorntons. I knows that.

"My folks was black, black as I is. Pa was stocky, guinea man. Ma was heap the biggest. She was rawbony and tall. I love to see her wash. She could bend 'round the easier ever I seed anybody. She could beat the clothes in a hurry. She put out big washings, on the bushes and a cord they wove and on the fences. They had paling fence 'round the garden.

"Massa Tom didn't have a big farm. He had a lot of mules and horses at times. They raised some cotton but mostly corn and oats. Miss Liza Jane left b'fore us. We all cried when she left. She shut up the house and give the women folks all the keys. We lived on what she left there and went on raising more hogs and tending to the cows. We left everything. We come to Hernando, Mississippi. Pa farmed up there and run his blacksmith shop on the side. My parents died close to Horn Lake. Mama was the mother of ten

and I am the mother of eight. I got two living, one here and one in Memphis.
I lives wid 'em and one niece in Natchez I live with some.

"I was scared to death of the Ku Klux Klan. They come to our house one
night and I took my little brother and we crawled under the house and got up
in the fireplace. It was big 'nough fer us to sit. We went to sleep. We
crawled out next day. We seen 'em coming, run behind the house and crawled
under there. They knocked about there a pretty good while. We told the
folks about it. I don't know where they could er been. I forgot it been
so long. I was 'fraider of the Ku Klux Klan den I ever been 'bout snakes.
No snakes 'bout our house. Too many of us.

"I tried to get some aid when it first come 'bout but I quit. My
children and my niece take keer er me. I ain't wantin' fer nothin' but
good health. I never do feel good. I done wore out. I worked in the field
all my life.

"A heap of dis young generation is triflin' as they can be. They don't
half work. Some do work hard and no 'pendence to be put in some 'em.
'Course they steal 'fo' dey work. I say some of 'em work. Times done got
so fer 'head of me I never 'speck to ketch up. I never was scared of horses.
I sure is dese automobiles. I ain't plannin' no rides on them airplanes.
Sure you born I ain't. Folks ain't acting lack they used to. They say so
I got all I can get you can do dout. It didn't used to be no sich way.
Times is heap better but heap of folks is worse 'an ever folks been before."

Interviewer_____Mrs. Bernice Bowden

Person interviewed_____George Benson
                          Ezell Quarters, Pine Bluff, Arkansas
Age   80   Occupation _____Cotton Farmer

- -

"I was here in slavery days — yes ma'm, I was here. When I come here, colored people didn't have their ages. The boss man had it. After surrender, boss man told me I ought to keep up with my age, it'd be a use to me some day, but I didn't do it.

"I member the soldiers would play with me when they wasn't on duty. That was the Yankees.

"I was born down here on Dr. Waters' place. Born right here in Arkansas and ain't been outa Arkansas since I was born. So far as I know, Dr. Waters was good to us. I don't know how old I was. I know I used to go to the house with my mother and piddle around.

"My father jined the Yankees and he died in the army. I heered the old people talkin', sayin' we was goin' to be free. You know I didn't have much sense cause I was down on the river bank and the Yankees was shootin' across the river and I said, 'John, you quit that shootin'!' So you know I didn't have much sense.

"I can remember old man Curtaindall had these nigger dogs. Had to go up a tree to keep em from bitin' you. Dr. Waters would have us take the cotton and hide it in the swamp to keep the Yankees from burnin' it but they'd find it some way.

"Never went to school over two months in all my goin's. We always lived in a place kinda unhandy to go to school. First teacher I had was named Mr. Bell. I think he was a northern man.

"All my life I been farmin' — still do. Been many a day since I sold a bale a cotton myself. White man does the ginnin' and packin'. All I do is raise it. I'm farmin' on the shares and I think if I raise four bales I ought to have two bales to sell and boss man two bales, but it ain't that way.

"I voted ever since I got to be a man grown. That is — as long as I could vote. You know — got so now they won't let you vote. I don't think a person is free unless he can vote, do you? The way this thing is goin', I don't think the white man wants the colored man to have as much as the white man.

"When I could vote, I jus' voted what they told me to vote. Oh Lord, yes, I voted for Garfield. I'se quainted with him — I knowed his name. Let's see — Powell Clayton — was he one of the presidents? I voted for him. And I voted for McKinley. I think he was the last one I voted for.

"I been farmin' all my life and what have I got? Nothin'. Old age pension? I may be in glory time I get it and then what would become of my wife?"

Interviewer   __Mrs. Bernice Bowden__

Person interviewed   __Kato Benton__
          Creed Taylor Place, Tamo Pike

Age__78__   Pine Bluff, Arkansas

- -

"I was born in South Carolina before the War. I ain't no baby. I wasn't raised here. No ma'am.

"My daddy's name was Chance Ayers and my mammy's name was Mary Ayers. So I guess the white folks was named Ayers.

"White folks was good to us. Had plenty to eat, plenty to wear, plenty to drink. That was water. Didn't have no whisky. Might a had some but they didn't give us none.

"Oh, yes ma'am, I got plenty kin folks. Oh, yes ma'am, I wish I was back there but I can't get back. I been here so long I likes Arkansas now.

"My mammy give me away after freedom and I ain't seed her since. She give me to a colored man and I tell you he was a devil untied. He was so mean I run away to a white man's house. But he come and got me and nearly beat me to death. Then I run away again and I ain't seed him since.

"I had a hard time comin' up in this world but I'm livin' yet, somehow or other.

"I didn't work in no field much. I washed and ironed and cleaned up the house for the white folks. Yes ma'am!

"No ma'am, I ain't never been married in my life. I been ba'chin'. I get along so fine and nice without marryin'. I never did care anything 'bout that. I treat the women nice—speak to 'em, but just let 'em pass on by.

"I never went to school in my life. Never learned to read or write.
If I had went to school, maybe I'd know more than I know now.

"These young folks comin' on is pretty rough. I don't have nothin' to
do with 'em--they is too rough for me. They is a heap wuss than they was in
my day--some of 'em.

"I gets along pretty well. The Welfare gives me eight dollars a month."

Interviewer_____Samuel S. Taylor_____

Person interviewed_____James Bertrand_____
                1501 Maple Street, Little Rock, Arkansas

Age___68___

- - - - - - - - - -["Pateroles" Both and Father]- - -

"I have heard my father tell about slavery and about the Ku Klux Klan
bunch and about the paterole bunch and things like that. I am sixty-eight
years old now. Sixty-eight years old! That would be about five years
after the War that I was born. That would be about 1870, wouldn't it? I
was born in Jefferson County, Arkansas, near Pine Bluff.

"My father's name was Mack Bertrand. My mother's name was Lucretia.
Her name before she married was Jackson. My father's owners were named
Bertrands. I don't know the name of my mother's owners. I don't know the
names of any of my grandparents. My father's owners were farmers.

"I never saw the old plantation they used to live on. My father
never told me how it looked. But he told me he was a farmer—that's all.
He knew farming. He used to tell me that the slaves worked from sunup
till sundown. His overseers were very good to him. They never did whip
him. I don't know that he was ever sold. I don't know how he met my
mother.

"Out in the field, the man had to pick three hundred pounds of cotton,
and the women had to pick two hundred pounds. I used to hear my mother
talk about weaving the yarn and making the cloth and making clothes out of
the cloth that had been woven. They used to make everything they wore—
clothes and socks and shoes.

"I am the youngest child in the bunch and all the older ones are dead.
My mother was the mother of about thirteen children. Ten or more of them

were born in slavery. My mother worked practically all the time in the house. She was a house worker mostly.

"My father was bothered by the pateroles. You see they wouldn't let you go about if you didn't have a pass. Father would often get out and go 'round to see his friends. The pateroles would catch him and lash him a little and let him go. They never would whip him much. My mother's people were good to her. She never did have any complaint about them.

"For amusement the slaves used to dance and go to balls. Fiddle and dance! I never heard my father speak of any other type of amusement.

"I don't remember what the old man said about freedom coming. Right after the War, he farmed. He stayed right on with his master. He left there before I was born and moved up near Pine Bluff where I was born. The place my father was brought up on was near Pine Bluff too. It was about twenty miles from Pine Bluff.

"I remember hearing him say that the Ku Klux Klan used to come to see us at night. But father was always orderly and they never had no clue against him. He never was whipped by the Ku Klux.

"My father never got any schooling. He never could read or write. He said that they treated him pretty fair though on the farms where he worked after freedom. As far as he could figure, they didn't cheat him. I never had any personal experience with the Ku Klux. I never did do any sharecropping. I am a shoemaker. I learned my trade from my father. My father was a shoemaker as well as a farmer. He used to tell me that he made shoes for the Negroes and for the old master too in slavery times.

"I have lived in Little Rock thirty years. I was born right down here in Pine Bluff like I told you. This is the biggest town—

a little bigger than Pine Bluff. I run around on the railroad a great
deal. So after a while I just come here to this town and made it my
home."

TITLES IN THE

SLAVE NARRATIVES SERIES

FROM APPLEWOOD BOOKS

ALABAMA SLAVE NARRATIVES
ISBN 1-55709-010-6 • $14.95
Paperback • 7-1/2" x 9-1/4" • 168 pp

ARKANSAS SLAVE NARRATIVES
ISBN 1-55709-011-4 • $14.95
Paperback • 7-1/2" x 9-1/4" • 172 pp

FLORIDA SLAVE NARRATIVES
ISBN 1-55709-012-2 • $14.95
Paperback • 7-1/2" x 9-1/4" • 168 pp

GEORGIA SLAVE NARRATIVES
ISBN 1-55709-013-0 • $14.95
Paperback • 7-1/2" x 9-1/4" • 172 pp

INDIANA SLAVE NARRATIVES
ISBN 1-55709-014-9 • $14.95
Paperback • 7-1/2" x 9-1/4" • 140 pp

KENTUCKY SLAVE NARRATIVES
ISBN 1-55709-016-5 • $14.95
Paperback • 7-1/2" x 9-1/4" • 136 pp

MARYLAND SLAVE NARRATIVES
ISBN 1-55709-017-3 • $14.95
Paperback • 7-1/2" x 9-1/4" • 88 pp

MISSISSIPPI SLAVE NARRATIVES
ISBN 1-55709-018-1 • $14.95
Paperback • 7-1/2" x 9-1/4" • 184 pp

MISSOURI SLAVE NARRATIVES
ISBN 1-55709-019-X • $14.95
Paperback • 7-1/2" x 9-1/4" • 172 pp

NORTH CAROLINA SLAVE NARRATIVES
ISBN 1-55709-020-3 • $14.95
Paperback • 7-1/2" x 9-1/4" • 168 pp

OHIO SLAVE NARRATIVES
ISBN 1-55709-021-1 • $14.95
Paperback • 7-1/2" x 9-1/4" • 128 pp

OKLAHOMA SLAVE NARRATIVES
ISBN 1-55709-022-X • $14.95
Paperback • 7-1/2" x 9-1/4" • 172 pp

SOUTH CAROLINA SLAVE NARRATIVES
1-55709-023-8 • $14.95
Paperback • 7-1/2" x 9-1/4" • 172 pp

TENNESSEE SLAVE NARRATIVES
ISBN 1-55709-024-6 • $14.95
Paperback • 7-1/2" x 9-1/4" • 92 pp

VIRGINIA SLAVE NARRATIVES
ISBN 1-55709-025-4 • $14.95
Paperback • 7-1/2" x 9-1/4" • 68 pp

* * * * * * * * * * * * * * * *

IN THEIR VOICES: SLAVE NARRATIVES
A companion CD of original recordings
made by the Federal Writers' Project.
Former slaves from many states tell
stories, sing long-remembered songs,
and recall the era of American slavery.
This invaluable treasure trove of oral
history, through the power of voices of
those now gone, brings back to life the
people who lived in slavery.
ISBN 1-55709-026-2 • $19.95
Audio CD

* * * * * * * * * * * * * * * *

TO ORDER, CALL 800-277-5312 OR
VISIT US ON THE WEB AT WWW.AWB.COM